BASS FISHING
Simplified

By
Bob Gooch

Atlantic Publishing
Tabor City, NC

Copyright 1993 by
Bob Gooch

First Printing 1993

Published by
Atlantic Publishing Company
Tabor City, NC 28463

Library of Congress Card Number 93-073904

ISBN 0-937866-43-1

Printed in the United States of America
by
Atlantic Publishing Company
Tabor City, North Carolina 28463

Cover design by Robbie Walker

To Pam and Pat

Other Books by the Author

The Weedy World of the Pickerels
Squirrels and Squirrel Hunting
Bass Fishing
In Search of the Wild Turkey
Coveys and Singles
Land You Can Hunt
Spinning for Trout
Virginia Hunting Guide
Virginia Afield
Virginia Fishing Guide
The Bird Hunter's Book
Hunting Boar, Hogs, and Javelina

CONTENTS

ACKNOWLEDGMENTS

Where do you begin when you try to thank the thousands of fellow anglers you've fished with over the years? So many have shared their knowledge and experiences that listing them all would take entirely too much space in a book of this kind. But they know who they are and if I omit them here, I hope they will understand. After all, I caught my first bass back in the days of the Great Depression. My brother Jack was with me on that fishing trip—and on many others in my early years. He rarely fishes anymore, but potentially he could be a good one. He caught a real lunker long before I did.

In later years there was Bill Snead of Virginia who introduced me to smallmouth bass fishing in the James River, one of the best in the nation. Fellow Virginian Woo Daves, a successful professional bass angler and an expert on fishing for tidal bass, has been a constant source of information when I wanted to write about the bass of the brackish waters.

Jim South of Southwest Virginia, an expert deep reservoir angler, opened up some of the secrets to fishing the big reservoirs which we'll touch on lightly here. If I could find the time he, would willingly teach me more. So would his son, Dr. Gregg South.

My wife Ginny has never been an angler, but she has shared many trips with me, content to shoot pictures, read a book, or just be good company. She's a fine outdoor companion and has followed me all over the North American continent, and even to Europe on fishing expeditions. She probably doesn't realize how much I am indebted to her.

Companions, game wardens, guides, lodge owners, and fellow outdoor writers have over the years unselfishly shared their knowledge. To one and all I humbly say, "thank you."

Bob Gooch
Troy, Virginia

Preface:

The polished hull of the sleek bass boat glittered in the bright lights of the arena, a big 150-horsepower outboard motor riding its stern. Lush carpeting covered the fore and aft casting decks. Between them was the cockpit or driving console and a host of modern electronic fishing aids. It was a honey, a real fishing machine, and the youngster's eyes widened perceptibly as he slowly circled the boat.

"Wow, Dad!"

Dad was impressed, very much so—but then he spotted the $20,000 price tag and shook his head.

"Too rich for my blood, son. Guess we'll have to stick with bluegills and crappie."

With that exchange, father and son disappeared in the enthusiastic crowd gathered at the annual outdoor show.

I was stunned. I wanted to plunge into the crowd, corner the young father, and get him aside for a few minutes.

"You don't have to own that expensive rig to be a bass fisherman," I wanted to tell him. "No reason to limit your fishing to bluegills and crappie. Please don't make bass fishing that complicated."

But I was too late. The milling crowd had swallowed them up. My opportunity had vanished.

The very thought that those obviously novice anglers would pass up the chance to fish for America's favorite game fish because they couldn't afford an expensive bass boat bugged me throughout the day. I found myself constantly coming back to that thought. Occasionally my thoughts would wander back to my own early angling years when even passable fishing tackle was hard to come by. I was well into my teens before I acquired my first casting reel, but in the meantime I had caught countless bass. So had my handful of fishing friends

Initially, we hadn't even owned cane poles, relying instead upon slender cedar poles cut in the spring when the sap was running so we could peel off the bark. I suspect our fishing lines were little more than strong cord, and I know we used bottle corks for floats. Nuts, washers—all kinds of objects served as weights. We did buy hooks, however at about a penny each. And we caught bass.

And here was a budding angler ready to turn his back on one of the grandest fish to fin America's waters because he couldn't afford a bass boat! Furthermore, he was going to deprive his eager son of the same opportunity.

Now I have nothing against bass boats. They have been a boon to bass fishing, particularly on the big, deep impoundments that provide so much of our fishing today. Bass boats were designed by folks who know bass fishing, people who quickly saw the value of foot-operated trolling motors that left both hands free to fish, who know the advantage of the comfortable casting platforms and the high seats, and the edge various electronic fishing aids offer the angler. They knew what they were doing.

But you don't need a bass boat to catch bass. In fact, some of the very best bass fishing waters in America are much too small for a bass boat.

Forgive me for returning to my early angling years for another illustration, but it was long after I had acquired my first casting tackle that I set foot in a boat. There were no boats in the farming community where I grew up. Still, my friends and I took hundreds of bass wading little creeks, occasionally making the long hike to the river where we fished from the banks, and somehow made our way along the brushy shoreline of a nearby millpond to cast to inviting bass waters.

It is not my intent to dwell here on the bass fishing I knew as a country lad, but it does help drive home my point that bass fishing need be neither complicated nor expensive. And you don't need a bass boat.

The bass today, both the largemouth and smallmouth as well as the less known Kentucky or spotted bass, is no different than its ancestors of 40 years ago. The big difference today is that there are more of them, and many more good fishing holes.

Outdoor magazines and television shows tend to dwell on the big waters and on the complicated and more expensive ways to catch bass. The newcomer is lured into the mistaken belief that he must put a second mortgage on his home so he can buy a fancy boat before he can take up bass fishing. Many of them, instead, simply throw up their hands as did that young father at the local outdoor show.

That impression is wrong, so wrong that I feel a compelling urge to correct it. There is a need to simplify bass fishing, to bring it down to a level that is within the reach of people from all walks of life irrespective of their rung on the economic ladder.

Bass are found in all of the fifty states except Alaska. Good fishing is seldom far away. How many game fish can you say that of? Even the ambitious trout management plans of the state fisheries agencies cannot make the trout available to much of the South. Trout fishing for many means a trip of several days at the least. Fishing for muskies, pike, and walleyes is spreading, but these fish are still not readily available to many anglers. But not so the bass, particularly the largemouth. Only the various panfish such as the bluegill and crappie can approach it for availability.

Possible bass waters are almost endless—beaver ponds, drainage ditches, farm ponds, millponds, potholes, roadside ditches, small creeks, small impoundments, the bigger rivers, and so on. And then there are the big natural lakes and the big artificial ones that dot the country in the form of flood control, hydroelectric, and water supply reservoirs. These are challenging waters, but for the beginning angler best placed in the future temporarily.

Catching a fine game fish so readily available should not be a complicated matter. It should be fairly simple, fun, relaxing, and fairly inexpensive. Fortunately that is generally the case.

Bass fishing can be simplified.

Chapter I
What Tackle?

Give me ten bucks and I can outfit you with the bare necessities in the way of fishing tackle, tackle with which you can go out and catch some bass. And you will probably have enough change left to buy the needed bait. It won't be fancy tackle, the kind you will want to spend the rest of your bass fishing career with, but it will catch bass for you — plenty of them. Get you started. Some very successful bass fishermen never get beyond the cane pole.

I checked in a tackle shop the other day and noticed plain bamboo fishng poles on sale for something in the $4 range. They were broken down into sections and fitted with ferrules so they could be easily transported and then assembled when you are ready to fish. To compliment the simple cane pole you need about 10 feet of 8 or 10-pound test monofilament line, a half dozen split-shot sinkers a half dozen fishing hooks in sizes 2 to 4, and a couple of plastic floats approximately an inch in diameter.

To rig your fishing tackle, fasten the monofilament line securely well back from the tip of the rod, wind it around the pole to the tip, and secure it well at the tip. The reason you begin back from the tip is the possibility you may hang a lunker that could break the tip — and take off with your rig. Thread the monofilament line through one of the floats, or snap the float on the line. Using an improved clinch knot, tie one of the hooks to the end of the line, and clamp on one of the split-shot sinkers. You may need several depending upon what kind of bait you use. If you fish with live minnows several may be required to keep the minnow from swimming to the surface instead of staying down in the water where a feeding bass will locate it. Experiment.

1

Yes, I caught my first bass on such tackle. The rod was a slender red cedar, however, cut in the spring when the sap was running so you could peel off the bark. And instead of a modern monofilament line we used, I believe, either silk or linen. I'm not sure what served as sinkers, Possibly some rusty nuts or screws. Hooks I bought for a penny each at a nearby country store. The profit must have been pretty good on those hooks. Even today they sell for little more! I suspect I used ordinary garden worms to take my first few bass, all largemouths. Later my friends and I learned that small live minnows made better bait. We caught them in a small creek that ran through my family's farm. Even today I insist there are few greater thrills in fishing than watching a dancing bobber and suddenly see it disappear below the surface.

Even President Roosevelt fished with a cane pole.

Young bass fisherman beginning his fishing career
in a small creek with a cane pole.

Later on I fashioned a crude fishing lure from a section of the same red cedar, copying from a mail-order catalog one that caught my eye. I removed the hook, sinker, and plastic float from my rig, tied on the lure, and with some friends headed to the headwaters of a millpond we kids had permission to fish. Ignoring the taunts from my friends, I stood back from the shore, stuck my pole a few feet over the water, and started slowly working the lure. Wham! A scrappy bass came from somewhere and smacked my crude lure. Following a quick tussle, I triumphantly swung the flopping bass ashore.

I tell you this not to suggest that you should begin your own bass fishing career so austerely, but rather to illustrate how simple and inexpensive bass fishing can be. I learned to fish back in the Great Depression. Even the ten

A lone bass among a catch of bluegills. Some anglers catch their
first bass while fishing for panfish.

dollars I'm suggesting now would have been a sizeable outlay then. I doubt if I had as much as a lone dollar invested in my original bass fishing tackle. The cost of hooks was insignificant, nuts or something similar served for sinkers, and ordinary bottle corks made fine floats. I suppose I bought some fishing line, or may even have substituted some other kind of line.

Though I caught countless bass on that tackle, I soon got the bug for something more sophisticated — particularly after landing that first bass on my crude lure. Incidentally, I still have that old lure.

This was before the days of spinning tackle in America and to step up I had two choices — bait-casting tackle or fly-fishing tackle.

The lone lure I had fashioned was a crude copy of a bait-casting plug as they were called in those days. Now crankbait is a more popular word. With some modest profits from an after-school trapline, I bought a steel casting rod, a cheap quadruple multiplying bait-casting reel, and a spool of silk casting line. I was also able to add a few wooden plugs to my collection of tackle.

The reel didn't have a level-wind guide, but I was able to handle that with a finger. And that line! What I hadn't learned was that silk line had to be dried thoroughly everytime you used it. Otherwise it would rot quickly. I learned that the hard way when I tried to cast one of my prize lures only to have the line snap. The lure sailed across the pond and ended up in a tangle of vines. I never found it.

Later I was able to assemble an inexpensive fly-fishing outfit and some cork popping bugs.

I caught bass on both the bait-casting and the fly-fishing tackle, and advanced as a bass angler.

If I were in the same shoes today, I would temporarily forget about the casting and fly-fishing tackle and turn to spinning tackle.

If we caught bass in the early days, we simply cut a forked branch from some streamside sapling, cut all but a couple of inches from one fork and left about 18 inches on the other fork. This was our stringer. We ran the long fork behind the gills and out of the mouths of our fish and marched proudly home with them. This was long before the days of catch-and-release. In fact, we were expected to bring home some fish for the table and we usually did. Today I would add an inexpensive chain stringer to my simple fishing tackle.

Neither bait-casting nor fly fishing are difficult to master, or at least to become proficient enough with to catch bass, but spinning is much easier to master. You don't enounter the backlash that is often the nemesis of the bait caster, particularly the beginner. Today, however, modern bait-casting reels have antibacklash features that tend to minimize this problem. The fly-fishing problem the beginner encounters is blending the flow of the line with the rod and getting out decent casts. The secret is to match the line and rod and ride out your backcast before shooting the line foreward. It takes practice. You also need plenty of room for your back cast, a problem confined to fly fishing.

The beauty of spinning is that, unlike the casting reel on which the spool spins as the line is peeled off, the spinning reel spool is stationery. The line simple peels off the spool as the lure takes it through the air. Spinning is the easiest of the several methods to master and in some cases the best choice for a particular kind of bass fishing. Some of the top bass fishing professionals use spinning tackle almost exclusively.

Line twist is the major problem with spinning, but it can be minimized by using swivels when fishing lures that revolve.

There are two kinds of spinning reels, the open-faced and closed-faced. Many beginners seem to chose the closed-faced reels, but I feel this is a mistake. They are called push-button reels because the line is controlled by the thumb on the casting hand which holds down a button until the angler is ready to release his lure. When the thumb is lifted the line is freed to follow the flight of the lure.

The line is enclosed on the closed-face reel whereas it is exposed on the open-faced one. Generally you can get better accuracy and more distance with the open-faced reel.

The forefinger on the casting hand controls the line when the open-faced reel is used, and this seems to give the angler a more sensitive touch.

The beauty of spinning tackle is the wide variety of lures and the various weights of lures the angler is able to use. Granted there are some situations in which bait-casting tackle of even fly-fishing tackle might be more appropiate, but most can still be handled with spinning tackle.

Simply going from a heavy line to a lighter one will allow you to cast lighter lures. Over the years I've seen bass anglers fish everthing from live bait to crankbaits on spinning tackle — and even plastic worms.

So what kind of spinning tackle should you buy?

Let's begin with the rod. First the material. Buy one of graphite if you can afford it. The price range is wide and generally you get what you pay for, but a good graphite rod can be purchased inexpensively in most tackle shops. Still, some good rods are made of fiberglass, or a combination of fiberglass and graphite. They are generally the less expensive rods, and durable. I've got some fiberglass rods I've owned for years and they are as good as new. Graphite is lighter and generally a bit more sensitive. Shop a little. The price varies considerably between the various retail outlets. I would go with a 6-foot rod and I would want a reasonably flexible tip, not too willowly, but flexible enough to handle a variety of lures. Such a spinning rod won't be the best for all bass fishing needs, but it will handle most of them at least adequately. Generally, those labeled medium-action fit this description. As you continue to fish for bass the various needs in rods will become evident and you can add to your battery of rods as your finances allow. In the meantime you will catch a lot of bass.

If you have the money to invest heavily in tackle put it in a good spinning reel. Just about any reel will function for awhile, but eventually the cheaper ones will develop

A happy young angler with
a good largemouth bass.

problems, particularly with the bail. You don't want an ultralight reel for bass, nor do you want a heavy one — possibly more appropriate for salmon or steelhead. Look for something in the 7 to 9-ounce range.

Rod and reel. Your major investment, but you'll need good line and plenty of it as most lines develop twists eventually and have to be discarded. Depending upon how much you fish, the line should be changed annually at the miminum. The size of the line is always debatable, but remember that as a general rule the lighter the line the better you can cast — get longer casts. I would suggest an 6 to 8-pound test line. If the rod has a flexible tip the 6-pound test line should be fine.

Beyond the rod, reel, and line are various accessories, but let's look at lures first. Topwater baits such as the Tiny Torpedo are popular and you should own a few, and also crankbaits that can be fished reasonably deep. These lures ofen have plastic lips that make them dig toward the depths as they are reeled in. You will also need a few spinnerbaits, and an assortment of plastic worms and grubs with a selection of grub or worm hooks to fish them on. You will need a few worm sinkers that you run your line through before tying it to a worm hook, and a few leadhead hooks for grubs.

Remember you are fishing a medium action-spinning rod and 6 to 8-pound test line so you want to stay away from the heavier lures and weights. Sizes ranging from 1/16 to 1/2 ounce should fill you initial needs. The heavier lures found in just about all tackle shops are intended for use on bait-casting tackle. Stay away from those 1-ounce lures for the present. Wait until you get into bait-casting.

Of course, you need something to store and transport the tackle you will accumulate — even initially. Even a day pack will work temporarily. Just pick up a couple of small plastic boxes to store lures in. Plastic holders that camera film come in are fine for hooks, sinkers, and other odd bits of tackle. Eventually, you will want a tackle box, but that can wait.

Carrying the fish presents a problem. You probably won't want to resort to the forked stick as I did in my early days. An ordinary fish stringer is fine, and a good one costs very little. It will last for years — or until you lose it. Get the ones with safety snaps for holding individual fish. With these you can string the fish through both lips and they will live for hours if kept in cool, fresh water.

Nail clippers for cutting line are handy, and cost less than a dollar at any drug store, and a pair of ordinary pliers from your tool kit will come in handy. Bring the needle-nose kind if you have them.

I like a towel for drying my hands after I have handled a fish or dipped them into the minnow pail for bait. And yes, bait. You will need something to carry it it. A discarded tin can is fine for worms, or simply leave them in the container they come in if you buy them at a bait shop. You want to keep your minnows alive and lively. For this you'll need a container. Any pail that doesn't leak will work, but it should have a cover to keep the minnows from jumping out. You'll probably have enough left out of that ten bucks to buy an inexpensive styrofoam bucket. It's a fine way to carry minnows, crayfish, or other natural bait you want to keep in water.

While spinning is relatively new to America, fly fishing is not only the oldest form of fishing in America, but also in the world. There's a place in bass fishing for the fly fisherman, particularly for the angler who likes to fish with popping bugs, cork-body lures with concave faces that pop noticeably when moved rapidly across the surface of the water. The elite of the fly fishing ranks often turn up their noses at popping bugs because, unlike the tiny flies they like to fish with, the larger bugs offer wind resistance which hampers the cast. Even so fishing popping bugs on the fly rod can be an extremely effective way to take bass feeding on the surface in shallow water. In fact, I know one bass angler who will fish no other way. Not surprisingly he catches a lot of bass.

The thing to keep in mind about fly fishing for bass is that you cast the line, not the lure. The reel does little more than hold the line, though some fly fishermen like to fight their bass with the reel.

By comparison bait-casting is relatively new. I believe it originated in America whereas both fly fishing and spinning came from the Old World, spinning as late as the late 1940's.

Bait-casting is popular among expert anglers because of the control it allows them. Casting accuracy can be a joy once the angler masters this kind of angling.

Whereas the spinning spool remains stationary, the spool on the bait-casting reel revolves as the weight of the lure pulls the line from the reel. In the old days it was necessary to thumb the fast-spinning reel carefully to prevent the revolving spool from overrunning the line and causing it to run back on the spool creating an impossible backlash.

This is a bird's eyeview of bass fishing tackle. Stand by for more indepth treatment in future chapters. The thing to remember here is that you can catch bass with very inexpensive tackle.

Chapter II
Open-Face Spinning Tackle

We've already taken a quick look at spinning tackle and explained the difference between open-face reels and closed-face ones. Here we will limit our discussion to the open-face reel and the tackle that fits it. It may be slightly more complicated than the push-button, closed-face type, but it is not difficult to master fairly quickly. Besides it is much more flexible.

Consider the weight of the reel. This may vary from 5 to 6 ounces to more than 20. The very light ones are generally known as ultralight reels. They are a joy to fish with on light tackle, but not rugged enough for a long season of bass fishing in various kinds of water and under a variety of conditions.

At the other end of the spectrum, we have the heavy reels in the 20-ounce class, reels built for saltwater fishing or for salmon, steelhead, striped bass or other heavy freshwater fish. They were not meant for bass fishing even for the lunker largemouth bass.

Having eliminated the very light and very heavy reels let's settle on something the middle range, say a reel in the 7 to 9-ounce range. Such a reel will handle a great variety of lures and stand up well under heavy fishing pressure.

Also look at the gear ratio, the number of times a single turn of the reel handle will circle the reel spool with line. Remember the spinning reel remains stationery, but the gears in the reel wind the line on the spool. Gear ratio can range from 4 to 7, but most are in the 5 to 6- ratio range,

A family fishing with open-face spinning tackle. (Mercury Marine photo).

and entirely adequate. The gear ratio determines the speed at which a lure will be retrieved in the hands of the average angler. A reel with a 6-gear ratio is going run the lure faster than one with a 4-gear ratio. For most fishing conditions the gear ratio is of minor importance, but it's well to know the ratio of your reel.

Reel line capacity is another consideration. Some reels, for example, may hold 150 yards of 8-pound test line. Obviously, the same reel will hold more yards of 6-pound test line. Line capacity, however, is seldom a problem in bass fishing. I've never had a fish run all of the line from my reel. It's good, however, to know the capacity of your reel for a given size line. Line capacity can vary from less than 100 yards to well over 250, depending to a degree upon the size of the line, but the size of the reel also is a factor.

Now turn to the fishing rod rack. The choices can

befuddle the beginning angler, but make a few mental notes and then check the various possibilities. On the better rods the vital statistics are listed on the butt section of the rod just beyond the forward grip.

You'll find spinning rods ranging in length from about 5 feet all the way up to 9 or 10 feet. Forget the long sticks. They are intended for salmon or steelhead. The average bass rod will be in the 6 to 8-foot range, and for a beginning I would lean toward the 6-foot rod. There are several things to consider. The shorter the rod the handier it is going to be to handle in tight quarters such as a river with lots of bank foliage. You want to also consider your fishing companion who shares a boat with you, particularly when fishing from a small boat, a 12 footer, for example. You don't want a long rod that's going to be a threat to him on a careless cast. Length, on the other hand, does give you greater casting range, but there are ways to compensate for this. For all-purpose bass fishing about the best compromise you will come up with is something like 5 feet, 9 inches to 6 1/2 feet. Such a rod will enable you to handle just about any bass fishing situation.

Action is even more important than length. Actions range from ultralight rods intended to cast tiny 1/16 to 1/4-ounce lures to medium-heavy ones built for lures up to an ounce in weight. Again the action is shown on the butt section of the better rods. Some might recommend a medium action for the beginner, but my recommendation is a medium-light rod. It should handle lures in the 1/8 to 5/8-ounce range. You can catch plenty of bass on such lures. The lures that match the rod should also be shown on the butt section.

A reasonably flexible tip can be an advantage in fishing topwater bass lures, and such a tip takes little from fishing other lures. The natural reaction when a bass hits a topwater lure is to strike too quickly, possibly on sight rather than by feel. Too often the result is a lure snatched from the fish before it takes it in its mouth. A missed opportunity. The flexible tip flexes when the angler strikes, and this delays the movement of the lure the split second

13

the fish needs to take it. While the line capacity of the reel is of questionable importance, the size of the line a rod is built for is of utmost importance. This too should appear on the butt section of the rod. Most medium-light action rods will handle line in the 4 to 10-pound test strength. The heavier line is adequate for just about any bass fishing situation, an exception being heavy weeds or other cover where it is necessary to horse a good fish into open water. Generally, however, a sturdy 10-pound test line will do this. A good thing to remember about fishing lines is that the lighter the line the easier it is to cast. The thin line is also less likely to spook a wary bass, but there are limitations on how light you want to go. A 4-pound test line calls for a rod with a very flexible tip. Actually, if I wanted to fish line that light I would go to ultralight tackle. Fished on a stiff rod, the light line is likely to snap easily. Generally, I lean toward 6 or 8-pound test line when fishing with medium-light rods. Even then I would limit the lighter line to water that is generally open and clear of obstacles.

You might want to consider buying an extra reel spool, one loaded with 6-pound test, for example, and the other with 8-pound line. Switching spools is done easily and quickly if the situation calls for a different strength line.

Rod, reel, and line, the basic ingredients of spinning tackle.

But why spinning tackle? Why not bait-casting or fly-fishing tackle? Probably the best answer is that spinning is a good compromise between the two older methods of fishing. When I emerged from the cane-pole class too many years ago, I had only the two choices. I began with bait-casting tackle because there were bass in a nearby pond I had permission to fish occasionally. It was fine for the heavy lures of that period, but when I wanted to go to lighter lures, for smallmouth bass for example, I was out of luck. They could not be cast on that old solid steel casting rod. So I turned to fly fishing and accumulated an inexpensive rod, reel, and line.

Today, I would not have encountered that problem.

14

Open-face spinning tackle is easy to master.

The spinning angler clamps the line with his forefinger before releasing it at the end of his cast. (Daiwa photo).

Spinning tackle is the solution, a compromise of course, but a good one. With it an angler can cast both large and small lures — within reason. Add a split shot or two and it's amazing how light a lure you can cast on a spinning outfit.

That's why I recommend spinning tackle for the beginning bass angler.

Sure, spinning tackle has its limitations, but they are not severe enough to significantly hamper an angler's chances of success. The spinning angler does not enjoy the casting accuracy the bait-caster does, nor does he have the complete control over his lure. A crack bait-casting angler can drop a lure on the money with amazing accuracy. And because his finger is lightly thumbing the rapidly turning reel spool he can halt the flight of the lure at any moment. For example, suppose he wants to drop a lure very lightly on the water, so softly he won't spook a nearby bass. He can allow the lure to sail over the water just above the target and at the right moment clamp his thumb tightly on the revolving reel spool. When he does so, the lure will be halted in flight to flutter and drop lightly on the water. When done correctly, it's a pretty piece of angling. That, however, can come later in your career — after you have mastered spinning and are ready to move on.

The bait-caster can also get by with a much shorter rod. A 5 footer is typical and for real cramped quarters he can operate effectively with a 4-foot stick.

Spinning tackle is by far the best choice for fishing natural baits such as night crawlers or live minnows. With spinning tackle you can deliver a soft, swinging, cast that will not snap the bait free. This is not possible with bait-casting tackle, and the back cast of the fly fisherman can rip a bait free. Spinning tackle definitely favors the bait-fishing angler. It's by far his best choice.

Let's move on to terminal tackle, the end of your fishing line. What goes there except a hook or lure? For many anglers nothing. They don't like to hamper the delicate action of their lures with a snap or swivel. It's mostly a matter of personal choice, although I lean toward the school that favors tying the lure directly to the line.

The major advantage of a snap or snap swivel is that it facilitates changing lures. A better approach, however, is to simply snip the line at the lure with a pair of clippers (the fingernail kind will do fine) and tie on the new lure. This way you eliminate some worn line and prevent a break-off. The line tends to wear most heavily toward its terminal.

Neither a snap or tying the lure directly to the line will eliminate line twist completely. Line twist is probably more of a problem in spinning than bait-casting. It is no problem at all for the fly-fishing angler. A good swivel, and I emphasize good, can help in this respect.

Line twist can begin when the line is spooled on the reel if it is not done correctly. The best way, perhaps, is to have the line spooled on at the tackle shop where you buy it, but you can do it correctly at home or on the water. Run a pencil through the hole in the spool and have a friend hold the spool while you crank it on. Or if a friend isn't immediately available hold the pencil between your feet or knees. In either case run the line though your fingers so it will not spool loosely on the reel.

Even if the line is spooled on correctly, twist will eventually develop. This is particularly true if you fish lures that spin as they are retrieved. Natural baits also tend to create line twist, particularly if they are fished in a current or trolled. So accept the fact. Line twist is inevitable.

Eventually the only solution is to change lines. Discard the old one and spool on a new one. In the meantime you can slow the process with the use of a swivel if you like. It can be a swivel in combination with a snap, or a swivel alone. Some anglers use a short piece of slightly heavier line to serve as a shock leader. They tie this directly to their lure and connect the leader to the line with a swivel.

Sometimes a twisted line can be untwisted to a degree by removing the lure or any other terminal tackle such as a snap and letting the line out in a strong current. Running it out behind a fast-moving boat will also help, though I prefer the fast current of a stream. This simply prolongs the life of your line. Eventually, you will have to replace it. A badly twisted line can spoil a fishing trip.

Before you go fishing learn to cast. It's simple and you don't even need an instructor though any experienced angler can speed you along.

With your rod and reel assembled and a new line spooled on, you are just about ready to begin. Ideally, you should practice with a casting weight. They are available at most tackle shops. Just make sure you get one that matches your rod. Check the weight. If a weight isn't available use a lure of the appropriate weight.

Now you are ready to make your first cast. If a pond is handy you may want to utilize it to make it more realistic, but your back yard will work fine. Now crank the reel handle and wind in the line so about six inches is separating the casting weight from the tip of your rod.

I like to grasp the reel with the stem to the reel seat between three fingers of my casting hand and my thumb resting on the rod. This leaves my forefinger free to pick up the line and my other hand free to flip the bail open. Now with the line held firmly against the rod with the tip of my forefinger, I bring the rod back to the one o'clock position. Stop here. Bring it too far back and you are likely to send your lure arching high in the sky and over some tree branch you weren't even aware of. With the rod in the one o'clock position and your forefinger holding the line firmly in place, snap the rod forward and release the line at approximately ll o'clock. The power of the rod should send the casting weight or the lure merrily on its way.

18

Author with a good smallmouth bass taken on
open-face spinning tackle.

19

Don't worry about distance initially. Just get the feel of the rod and then you can concentrate on placing the lure on target and seeking more distance. A couple of hours of practice and you should be ready to go catch some bass.

A couple of pointers might help you along toward becoming an accomplished spinning angler. One thing to remember is long casts are not necessary. Accuracy, the ability to place your lure where you feel a bass might be waiting, is more important.

Also bear in mind that to gain distance you might want to consider leaving a bit more than six inches of line dangling from the end of your rod. On the other hand shorten that distance a couple of inches and you gain in accuracy.

Over the years you will learn about side casts and underhand casts. A side cast which sends the lure skimming just above the surface will help get your lure back under overhanging vegetation or even boat docks where bass love to hang out on hot days. Bass seek shade to loaf in when the weather is hot and sunny. An underhand cast is little more than an upward flip of the casting hand, a good trick for short casts in close quarters.

As you progress, improve your casting technique, and at the same time become more knowledgeable about the ways of the black bass, your spinning tackle with become almost a part of you. And as it does, you will learn the true joy of spinning for bass.

Chapter III
The Lures

Regardless of how he begins his bass fishing career, the serious angler is going to eventually switch to fishing with artificial lures. A worm fisherman initially? And then live minnows? It matters not, the fascination of fooling bass on artificial lures is just too strong. It is much of the lure of bass fishing.

I won't repeat the story of how I took my first bass on artificial lures fishing a plug of my own crude and limited design. It worked and I've been pitching artificial lures since. That doesn't mean that I don't occasionally go back to worms, live minnows, or some other natural bait. There are times when the situation dictates some kind of natural bait. We'll talk about natural baits in the next chapter.

Over the years I've learned, however, that day in and day out artificial lures will take more bass than natural baits. That's another good reason to fish them. Beginning anglers get caught up on casting lures, be it on a casting, fly fishing, or spinning rod, and soon learn that they can catch more bass than they have in the past when limiting themselves to natural baits. They do so primarily because they cover more water, much more. Oh, I know many bait anglers work the current with their baits, drifting them to waiting bass, but most simply bait up and fish the bottom of a likely pool until boredom eventually drives them to new water. Not so the artificial lure angler. He is constantly casting to new water and working his lure through every likely-looking spot. He spends very little time on unproductive water before moving on. He may work the shoreline, obstacles in the current of a stream, or even the cover afforded by boat docks. He doesn't miss a single piece of water that looks even slightly productive.

A good selection of bass lures—crankbaits, plastic grub, plastic worm, and modification of spinnerbait.

You already own a medium-light or a medium action spinning rod, one you have caught untold numbers of bass on while fishing natural baits. Now before you even look at an artificial lure, check the butt section of your rod and see what weight lures it is built to cast. Building your lure collection within the range of weights recommended will save you a lot of headaches down the road. My favorite spinning rod, a Daiwa medium-light action rod is built for lures in the 1/8- to 3/4-ounce range. Recommended line strength is 6 to 12 pounds. For lures in the lighter ranges I spool on 6-pound test line, and in fact rarely go above 8-pound test. No, I don't carry along a set of scales to weigh my lures! I check the weights before I buy them and am reasonably familiar with each lure. Slight deviations here and there are not going to make that much difference, but I do keep in mind the rod-to-lure ratios.

With that background we are just about ready to visit a tackle shop. But before we do so let's attempt to group broadly the various kinds of lures on the market. I like to think in terms of topwater or surface lures, diver-floaters, crankbaits, spinnerbaits, spoons, jigs, and soft plastic baits. Many of these lure types have been around for generations, particularly spoons. It was probably the original artificial lure. Crankbaits and spinnerbaits are new in name only. Crankbaits were called plugs in the old days and you may hear this still used. The spinnerbait closely resembles the old Shannon Twin Spinner, and the in-line spinner is not new by any means. Some anglers might include diver-floaters with crankbaits, but I like to consider them separately. They *are* different.

Probably the most popular of them all over the years has been the surface or topwater lure. In the old days they too were called plugs. One of the most popular of all time is the Hula Popper. It's still popular—and productive.

Surface lures are popular because they provoke the topwater strike, and a big old bass busting a popping or gurgling surface lure is one of the greatest thrills in fishing. Few moments are more heart-stopping. Some anglers refuse to fish with any other lure. "Never throw anything except a topwater plug," they'll declare. Modern bass angling has proved the futility of this. There are times when a topwater lure won't work, but some other lure might just keep the water churning with striking bass. Stock your tackle box with a few lures in each group *and use them.* They give you flexibility. Even though we don't know the reason why, there are times when bass will hit one lure and rarely nothing else. On the other hand there are times when they will seemingly hit anything that you cast. Those periods, unfortunately, are rare. Usually the angler has to cater to the fish, give them what they want.

Another old favorite in the topwater surface group is the Jitterbug. It was probably named for a style of dancing that was popular back in the 1930's and '40's. The lure has been around for a long time. The Jitterbug is a short chunky lure that floats, but it has a wide metal lip that gurgles when the lure is worked through the water. It never makes the popping sound of the Hula Popper, but it does get the attention of bass when it's fished properly and the fish are looking up for their food. New entries in the topwater category are the Pop-R which, like the Hula Popper, has a concave face that creates the popping sound when it is retrieved. Also relatively new is the tiny Torpedo, a surface lure with a propeller in back. It's particularly popular among smallmouth bass anglers. The Zara Spook is a favorite of some topwater anglers. It's a floater with limited action other than that the angler gives it with his rod. The Slap-Stick lure adds a new feature to topwater fishing with rattles that attract by sound and create vibrations in the water. Most of these surface lures come in various weights, including those appropriate for your medium-light action rod. You don't need to buy all of these lures initially, but study the various actions and choose one from each.

Now let's look at the floater-divers. Some include these with surface lures because they do float when not in motion, while others group them with crankbaits—I suppose because to fish them you crank them in with your reel. I prefer to consider them separately. Probably the best example of this class of bass lures is the famous Rapala, an import, but stocked in most tackle shops. The lure floats when not being retrieved, but plastic lips on the head of the lure cause it to dive and wobble when retrieved. The faster it is retrieved, the deeper it goes. This feature probably accounts for its inclusion by some in the crankbait category. Most floater divers are long and narrow, but there are exceptions. There are even chunky-body Rapalas that float to the surface when not in motion. The Wee-R is another float-diver of chunky build—even more so than the similar lure in the Rapala series. The beauty of these lures is that you can run them deeply or let them float to the surface where you can make them flutter like a dying minnow. The expert angler can do all kinds of things with the floater-divers.

Bass anglers coined the term crankbait, and it has since become one of the most popular bass fishing lures in America. There are dozens of them on the market and each offers something unique, but the beginning angler should be able to get away with two or three initially. To fish a crankbait you cast it out there and reel it rapidly in. some will float to the surface when inactive, but the crankbait was never intended to be a topwater lure. Lure manufacturers, however, have added floater-dive crankbaits to their lines. Common to most crankbaits are a stubby body and plastic lips of varying lengths. The longer the lip the deeper the lures will run when reeled in rapidly. The Wally Diver, for example, will run as deep as 30 feet, but it was designed with walleye, not bass, in mind. The Big-O was one of the earliest crankbaits, and it's still a good one. On the Big-O the eye was on the nose of the lure, but on many the eyes rest on the lips. Where it is placed depends upon how deeply the lure was intended to run.

When it comes to weight you have a wide choice in crankbaits. The Pee Wee Wart, for example, weighs just 1/5 ounce. Bombers may weigh as much as 3/4 of an ounce. The crankbait is one of the easiest bass lures to cast and detect a strike on. Bass often hook themselves when they hit a crankbait because of the usually two sets of treble hooks.

Many crankbaits have built-in rattlers that seem to get a bass's attention. A good example of this crankbait is the Rattlin' Flat Wart. Most are built to resemble fat minnows, or probably more nearly small members of the sunfish family that bass so often feed on. Others such as the Hot Craw resemble crawfish. The Rat-L-Trap is a thin crankbait that attempts to imitate shad, a favorite forage fish in big waters.

The most unlikely appearing bass catcher of them all is the spinnerbait. It's an awkward lure with a single hook covered by a skirt riding beneath a bright, reasonably large spinner—or spinners. Some have twin spinners. When I first looked at a spinnerbait I had absolutely no confidence in the lure. Even now I don't use them as much as I should, for it can be a deadly bait. Still, I'm always surprised when I catch a bass on a spinnerbait. Used as a buzz bait, it is retrieved rapidly across the surface, just fast enough to keep it from sinking. It leaves a noticeable wake, but when done correctly under the right conditions it can be deadly. A triangular-shaped wire separates the skirt-covered hook from the spinner or spinners, and the eye of the lure is at the apex of the triangle. Some spinnerbaits have trailer hooks behind the main hook. Some also have plastic or trailers of some other soft material. While the usual spinner is round or oblong, others come in a variety of shapes. Some spinnerbaits have plastic bodies instead of skirts. While any spinnerbait can serve as a buzz bait, there are on the market those built just for buzzing. Most have triangular blades with lips. You don't need to invest heavily in spinnerbaits initially. Get one each of several different styles and pick up some additional skirts and trailers to modify them.

In-line spinners where the spinner rides ahead of the skirt or hook, or on the same stem, are pretty much limited to small-mouth bass fishing. Some of these lures are very light, 1/32 ounces, for example, but intended for panfish or trout. Spinners in the 1/4-ounce range are best for bass. Good examples of this kind of lure are the Mepps spinners. Others include the Blue Fox, Panther Martin, and Rooster Tail. On some the stem runs directly through the end of the spinner. Panther Martin spinners are a good example.

In-line spinners made by Mepps.

Spoons have never been particularly popular among

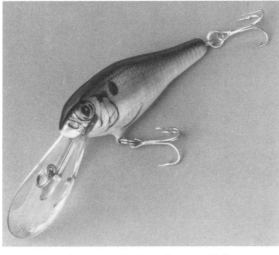

Long lip makes Bagley's Deeper Diving Bass 'n' Shad run deep when retrieved.

bass anglers. They are probably used mostly by smallmouth anglers and rarely by them. Among the spoons the best known is probably the age-old Daredevil in red and white. Over the years, however, it has probably caught more pike than it has bass. Probably a more popular bass spoon, particularly for smallmouths, is the Silver Minnow. In the old days pork rind was used to make spoons more enticing, but today plastic and rubber do just as well, and both are easier to store. Spoons are easy to cast, and the Silver Minnow is weedless, a real asset for the bass angler. I believe I would add a spoon or two to my bass tackle box, at least one of which would be red and white. I would also add a Silver Minnow or two.

Jigs. Now that's one that includes a great variety of lures from a simple bucktail to the pig-n-jig, one of bass angler Bill Dance's favorite lures for smallmouth fishing. Jigs are generally built on leadhead hooks. The lead provides the casting weight, and the hook is covered with a hair or rubber skirt. The pig-n-jig is usually clothed in a rubber skirt. Generally, jigs are reasonably weed-proof. Jigs can be very productive for a great variety of fish, though they are not as popular among bass fishermen as are some of the other classes of lures.

Now we come to plastic lures. While we discuss them last, they are by no means last in the hearts of bass anglers. In fact, they are the favorite of many successful

27

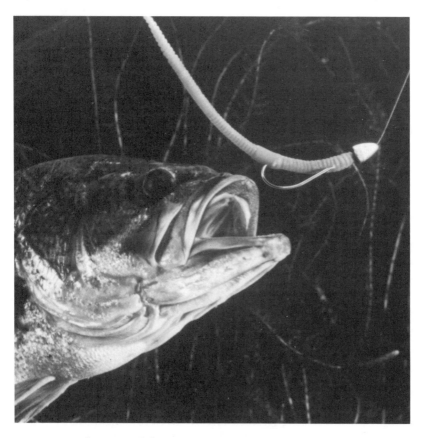

Largemouth bass prepares to take a plastic worm.

anglers. It's a different kind of fishing though. A bass will hit a crankbait and spit it out immediately if it is not hooked. The hard lure provides an instant warning that the lure is a fake. The soft plastic, on the other hand, apparently pleases the tastes of bass. They are often found in the stomachs of bass that are cleaned for the table. This means a different style of fishing. Rarely are the lures worked rapidly as is a crankbait. Nor is the strike by the angler the same. Fishing plastics is not too much unlike fishing natural baits. Some anglers like to let the fish take the lure and move off before striking. It's mostly a matter of personal choice, however, and some good anglers insist you should strike the moment you feel the fish. Take your choice. The thing to remember, however, is that the bass may swallow the plastic, and removing it will kill the fish. If you are a catch-and-release angler, strike immediately—before the lure is taken too deeply to remove.

The plastic worm revolutionized bass fishing, introduced an entirely new concept for catching the popular fish. It's slow fishing, a kind of fishing I had difficulty accepting. But it's productive, particularly during the warm summer months when the bass are deep and hard to find. Worms come in various lengths. I like the shorter ones, but they are available from about four inches up to eight or 10. Colors? The oil color is popular, and so is purple. But they come in a great variety of colors. So when you buy a pack get assorted colors. Worms traditionally are fished behind a lead sinker that is threaded on the line ahead of the worm. It is bullet-shaped with the back end concave so it fits tightly against the worm. It furnishes the casting weight and sinks the worm deep where summer bass are found most often. A great range of weights is available so pick those recommended for your rod, allowing a little for the weight of the worm. You also need special worm hooks. Ask for them if you experience trouble making a choice. You'll want fairly large hooks, something in the 1/0 to 5/0 range. Mix the sizes, and buy a fair number because you can lose a lot of hooks. Other methods include special worm rigs which contain a string of hooks and leadhead hooks which are more popular for fishing grubs and other kinds of plastic lures.

While worms are among the more popular of the plastic lures, grubs come in all kinds of forms. Some represent frogs and other aquatic life, but others simply are built to be enticing and really imitate nothing in particular. There are short worms with curly tails, lizards, crawfish, triple tails, bugs, tube worms, and so on. There's usually something new every season. Some of the trade names include Do Nothing Worms, Jelly Worms, Mister Twister, Tube Worms, and so on.

We haven't given much attention to color, but I like

those that imitate forage fish or other natural food. Still, you can't argue with chartreuse, orange, and other attractor colors that catch bass with amazing frequency.

Don't overload with too many lures, but select some good ones from each group and you'll have all you need to catch any kind of bass wherever it swims.

Chapter IV
Natural Baits

Possibly we should have discussed natural baits first and then followed with artificial lures. Beginning anglers usually resort first to natural baits and then go on to artificial lures. At least I suspect that's the case, and I doubt it will change.

But it's difficult to develop casting skills with natural baits. They simply will not hold up under the stress of continuous casting and retrieving. Natural baits call for adjustments in casting, but we will get to that later. That's why I covered artificial lures first, to promote the early development of casting techniques. Now let's get down to the basics of fishing with natural baits, what works best for bass, where to obtain it, and how to use it.

I don't recall my first bass. I do know it was a largemouth, because that was all that was available in the waters I fished as a tot. I do recall the first bass I caught on an artificial lure, but that was not my first bass. I am almost certain, however, that that first bucketmouth was taken on a worm. No, not the big nightcrawlers that are popular among bass anglers today, but a simple earthworm dug from the garden plot. Trout fishermen refer to them as garden hackle.

Earthworms, usually easy to obtain and thus inexpensive, can be a beginning. The problem is finding ones large enough to interest bass. The average earthworm is best used for panfish or trout — but bass will also hit them. It may not be the best natural bait, but a garden worm will serve to begin with.

You can't, to my knowledge, buy earthworms. You dig them with a hoe or spade. Garden plots are fine, but so is

31

any very fertile soil. Old barn sites are good. You can also gather them by turning over boards or flat rocks.

The old tin can of the barefoot boy will still serve as a container to store and carry the worms. They will keep better if you add some soil to the can. Put several inches on top of the worms. This keeps them from freezing in cold weather and from dying in hot weather. Once you begin fishing, you might want to dump out the soil. The worms will become more accessible.

As a kid I threaded the worm on my hook, making sure that the point was covered. For some reason, I felt that if the point of the hook was visible the bass wouldn't take it. Was I ever wrong! You want to present the worm squirming and as natural as possible. This means running the hook through its collar and letting it wiggle. When it refuses to do so, remove it and put a fresh one on.

In stream fishing, be it for largemouth, smallmouth, or spotted bass, the best approach is to drop the worm in the current and let it go with the flow. Stream fish look to the current for their food and a worm, floating and squirming by, can look mighty inviting to a hungry bass.

I like to add a split shot or two to get the worm down in the current and add a little casting weight, but you may want to try fishing a weightless line. Experiment. You can get out a fair cast with just the weight of the baited hook. This is particularly true if the worm is fairly large. Some earthworms approach nightcrawler size.

The usual snappy cast, the forward snap of the wrist, won't work for fishing worms — or most baits. You might get out a cast or two, but you'll soon snap the bait free and send it flying across the water. You have to deliver a very soft cast when fishing bait. You get your entire casting arm into the cast more, a swinging action. Actually a modified side cast might be better. Experiment until you are able to get the baited hook out there safely without out loosing it.

I don't like to cast a worm downstream and work it back against the current. The worm should move with the current, not against it. One good approach is to cast diagonally across the current and slightly upstream and let the current sweep the lure downstream while you maintain a reasonably tight line. You can also cast directly upstream if you like, but it means reeling in line almost constantly as the bait works its way back toward you.

Nightcrawlers are a much better choice for bass fishing than earthworms. They are larger and seem to stay lively longer. They are on sale at most tackle shops and at many country stores in fishing country. You see them advertised as "Canadian nightcrawlers," and they are fairly expensive as they have to be refrigerated to keep them alive. You can also collect your own by combing rich soil after dark. Use a flashlight and search golf courses and other richly fertilized areas, well-fertilized lawns for example. Get permission first, of course. Immediately following a rain they often come out in the daytime, but the sun and heat will send them back into the ground. Place them in moss in a tight container and nightcrawlers will keep for days in a home refrigerator.

Other possible worms include red wigglers and meal worms. They too are small and would come as a second choice to night crawlers.

Fishing worms in lakes or ponds where there is little or no current is a different matter. I suspect that first bass I caught on a worm was fished below a bobber. Bobbers are still a possibility though experienced bass anglers rarely use them.

The advantage of a bobber is that it keeps the worm suspended in the water, squirming and wiggling for all bass to see. And you can catch a lot of bass this way. You might have to test several different depths. You can do this by moving the bobber up or down on your line. Maybe it's a holdover from the old days as a kid, but I enjoy fishing with a bobber. Seeing that bobber come suddenly to life and the disappear beneath the surface remains one of the greatest thrills in fishing.

More experienced bass anglers might like to fish with a tight line, watching the line for a bite or detecting it by feel as they would an underwater artificial lure. They may work the worm slowly along the bottom or cast it out, let it sink slowly, reel in, and cast again. That way you cover more water than when using a bobber.

Despite the worm's effectiveness as a bass bait, a lively minnow is better. It didn't take me long to go from worms to minnows, of which there was an abundance in the small creek that ran through the family farm in Virginia. Dead minnows will also take bass, but they are not as productive as live ones — or better, lively ones. I don't believe size makes a lot of difference, but go into a bait store and you'll usually find several tanks all

A handy way to keep live minnows alive and healthy. (Plano Molding Company photo.)

offering different sizes. They may range from little one inchers to large ones for striped bass or even big largemouths. Some are six inches or more in length.

You can get a debate going as to the best way to hook minnows, through the lips or through the back. I feel it depends mostly upon how you plan to fish them. If you are going to bait up and drop the minnow straight down and suspended a certain depth beneath a bobber, then I believe hooking the minnow through the back just to the rear of the dorsal fin is the best way to do it. You have to be very careful that you don't hit the backbone. This would kill the bait almost immediately. On very small minnows there's precious little room to work in. For the little ones hooking them through the mouth might be better. If you do hook them through the lips make sure the hook goes through both lips otherwise the minnow will soon drown.

Just as in the case of worms, it's best to use the current to fish minnows in the streams. Here you will of necessity

34

have to hook the bait through both lips. A minnow, hooked through the back and pulled through the water, is going to look awkward. It will also most likely pull free very quickly. You can fish minnows just as you would worms casting diagonally across the current and letting them flutter and struggle in the current, or you can cast them upstream and allow them to work back toward you. In addition, a minnow pulled upstream in the current is not unnatural. Let it flutter and appear to be struggling with the current.

Incidentally, strikes on natural baits, worms, minnows, or whatever, often come as the bait drifts out of the current at the end of a drift. The fish apparently fear the bait is attempting to escape the current and get away.

You can buy minnows at most bait or tackle shops, or you can catch your own. Just check the local regulations having to do with catching small fish for bait. The quickest way to catch them is with a small seine. Work it along the shallows of a lake, or better still, find a small stream and work the seine through the pools. Often you can get all the bait you need in a single sweep of the seine. Don't take more than you need. Those little minnows are important to the life in that stream, and you don't want to risk wiping them out, though that's a remote possibility. You might want to return any you don't use to the waters from which you caught them.

Minnow traps are another good way to catch minnows for bait. These are net wire containers with funnels in each end. The minnows can swim into the trap, but have trouble escaping because the the way the funnel is built. Bait such a trap with bread crumbs, lower it into a pool in a creek or the shallows of a lake or pond. Go back a few hours later and you may have all you want. Most live-minnow anglers own seines or traps — or both.

Keeping the minnows alive and active can be a problem in warm weather. You have to change water frequently, using creek or spring water if possible. The water from a city water system may or may not harm the minnows. The only way you can find out is to test a few in it — or ask a fellow angler who lives in the same city or town. He may

35

A minnow trap is handy for catching live minnows for bait.

have already learned the hard way. I have no problem with my tap water, but I live in the country and my water comes from a deep well — untreated.   In any event keep a close eye on those minnows if you purchase them before a trip and have to hold them any length of time. Certainly, the best approach is to pick the minnows up from the bait shop on the way to your fishing waters.

Keeping the minnows alive during the course of a fishing trip is less of a problem. Some boats have built-in live wells that allow the water from the lake or stream to constantly refresh the water in the well. Minnow pails that you can sink over the side of the boat are also good — assuming, of course, that the weather is not so hot it warms the surface water above an acceptable level.   Then you might possibly attach a line to the pail and lower it even deeper in the lake. If you don't use one of these methods, buy a cheap styrofoam minnow pail, fill it with cool, fresh water, preferably from a stream, and put your minnows in it. They will keep much longer in the styrofoam pail than in a metal one — unless the metal one can be sunk in the lake. Keeping minnows alive and lively does take some time. Maybe that's why most anglers stick with artificial lures.

Line twist can be a problem when fishing natural baits, particularly when you work them in the current of a river. A good swivel might be a good idea to prevent this, though I must admit that I seldom use one. If my line becomes badly twisted I remove the hook and bait and let the line run out downstream in the current, the stronger the current the better. If it happens while you are fishing in a lake try running the line out behind your boat and making a fast run down the lake and back. Generally, however, I don't find this as effective as a good current in a fast stream.

Minnows and worms are probably the most popular two natural baits, but there are others equally as good. Take crayfish, or crawfish, for example. They are tough and a favorite of smallmouth bass anglers. They're just as good for other bass, and remain the preference of some bass anglers. Usually, you have to collect your own crayfish, and that's one reason they are not used more. The same seine that you use to catch minnows in a small stream will also catch crayfish. In fact, you usually catch a few while seining for minnows. If so, keep them in the pail with your minnows. They will live much longer. You can increase your crayfish catch by turning over stream-bottom rocks and stirring the critters up. They swim backward, so keep this in mind when trying to catch some moving ones. Crayfish are hooked through the tail.

Leeches are probably used less for bass than they are for walleyes, but they are a good bass bait. They inhabit most streams, and to catch them you can use a large metal can of some kind, dump almost any kind of meat in it, and put a cover of some kind on it, leaving just enough room for the leeches to enter the can. Sink the can in a stream and pull it out the next morning. The meat will be infested with leeches. To fish them they are hooked through the head.

Other lesser baits include crickets, grasshoppers, lo-

A pair of bass anglers work a seine for live minnows.

custs, and other large insects. Ever notice how bass leap out of the water in an effort to catch low-flying dragon flies? These baits will work in a pinch, but most anglers prefer crayfish or minnows for bass.

Mad toms, tiny catfish just a couple of inches long, are a favorite bait of smallmouth bass angler, particularly the stream anglers. They are tough, stay on the hook well, and live a long time. They are best collected by seining small streams at night when they are out. They spend most of they daylight hours under rocks and other cover on the bottoms of streams. Like most catfish they also have a sharp spine in the dorsal fin that can inflict a painful injury. They must be handled with care.

Handling natural baits can be messy. Both minnows and worms tend to be slimy, and you also get your hands wet. A small towel to dry your hands adds much to the comfort of the bait fisherman. For minnows you might also consider a tiny dip net, usually of wire, to remove them from the pail or live well. It's better than constanting dipping your hand in the water, particularly during cold weather.

The fisherman who cuts his angling teeth on natural baits will find himself going back to them occasionally throughout his long angling career. There's a certain fascination with collecting and using natural baits that never dies. I find myself often starting a new season with natural baits and gradually switching to artificials as the weather warms and the bass begin to move about more.

Natural baits are preferred by some experienced bass fishermen when the fish are deep — either in the heat of summer or the dead of winter.

The angler who doesn't know how to fish natural baits is not a complete fisherman.

Chapter V
Inexpensive and Handy Boats

You don't really need a boat to catch bass. I was well along in my teens before I even put a foot in a boat, but in the meantime I had taken hundreds of largemouth bass, some good ones. Even so I longed for a boat to fish from, one that would get me into water I couldn't otherwise reach. The desire just wouldn't go away. Something appealing about stepping into a boat, rowing or paddling out across water much too deep for wading, and catching some bass.

That desire was soon translated into action, and I got busy building a boat of whatever material I could scrounge. The result wasn't much, but some friends and I did put it in the headwaters of a local millpond we had permission to fish. The crudely constructed boat leaked initially, but we left it in the water long enough for the wood to swell and seal most of the leaks.

We caught some bass from that crude boat, learned a bit about building and handling a boat, and the rudiments of fishing from a boat. These early lessons have served me well over the years.

Today there are all kinds of inexpensive boats on the market that will meet the bass angler's needs. The major problem is settling on one that best fits those needs. There is probably no such thing as the ideal boat for all kinds of bass fishing, but some will come close enough for practical purposes.

I'll go out on a limb here and recommend a metal jon boat, the flat-bottomed ones that are popular among river fishermen. Depending upon whether you will do most of your fishing alone or with a companion, I would look at something in the 10 to 12-foot range. Buy one light enough

A light jon boat can be carried on the top of just about any vehicle.

to lift into the body of a pickup truck or to the cartop rack on the family sedan. Boats in the 100-pound weight range are about right. Stay away from bright colors. Aluminum is light and popular, and it will eventually fade to a dull finish. But ideally the boat should be painted a marsh green color, particularly if it will be used for hunting as well as fishing. The dull color will also be better for fishing. Fish tend to shy away from bright metal or brightly painted metal. Make sure the boat is fitted with oar locks, and has handles at both ends for ease in handling and lifting.

I have a little 3 1/2 horsepower motor that works fine on a small jon boat, but it's an old one. You can get more horsepower in lightweights today. You don't need too much horsepower, nor do you want a motor that's so heavy the boat will ride with the bow in the air. Ask the dealer for the manufacturer's recommendation — or better still take the boat and motor out to a local lake and test it. If the motor is too large, it will soon become obvious.

Most small outboard motors have built-in gasoline

40

tanks so you will need a gasoline tank for spare fuel. One that holds about three gallons of gasoline will serve you well. That plus the capacity of the motor tank will keep you going for a long time.

You aren't going to be able to launch your little boat and race to the other end of a lake, or miles up a river as do those in bass boats. You can, however, cover a lot of good fishing water. If you decide to move across the lake or miles upstream, it's a simple matter to put your boat back into your truck or on your cartop rack and drive to a launching ramp convenient to the water you want to fish.

There are a number of little attachments you can add to your boat that will add to the pleasure of fishing. Most marine supply stores have rings or hooks that can be attached to the boat. They are handy for fastening a fish stringer, for example, or possibly a line or even anchor ropes. You will also need at least one anchor, but two are better if you plan to do much fishing with minnows or other natural baits. A boat swinging on a single anchor can be frustrating. Ideally, one of the anchors should be on a pulley. Inexpensive ones are available for less than $20.

Seats are another option. You can buy those that clamp to the existing seats in the boat thereby adding a cushion and a back rest, or you can mount them on pedestals that are attached permanently to the boat. Seats are certainly not a necessity, and you can skip them for awhile if you like.

Now we come to the typical bass boat fittings. Most of them you can get along without — all of them in fact. But I would add a few. One thing I like is a foot-operated trolling motor mounted on the bow. It's a great convenience when fishing a shore line, a great place to take bass. You can stand there with both hands free to fish and cast as you work slowly along the shore. This is a real advantage if you fish alone, but also helpful when you have a partner. Both can fish with a minimum of attention being diverted to boat handling. In the old days this kind of fishing called for a guide or a pair of anglers, one to paddle the boat slowly while the other fished. Some anglers are even successful

41

in mounting a hand-operated trolling motor on the bow of their boats and operating that with a foot on the handle. You might want to try that. The hand-operated trolling motors are considerably less expensive than the foot-operated ones.

Another possible addition is a fish finder or depth finder. At the minimum these electronic aids read the depth for you, but the better ones also show fish at various depths. You can catch a lot of bass, however, without these electronic gadgets.

You will, of course, need a battery for your trolling motor. It might also serve for the fish-finding gear. Make sure you buy a trolling battery instead of a starting battery.

For traveling, a set of oars placed in the oar locks provide the best momentum, but there are times when a paddle is handy. You can actually use one of the oars as a paddle, but a regular canoe paddle is better.

If you don't own a pickup truck and dislike lifting the boat to the top of your sedan or station wagon then buy an

Many anglers like folding boats that can be carried on the roof of an automobile and unfolded at the fishing site. (Plano Molding Company photo.)

inexpensive trailer for your boat. The trailer, of course, adds dimensions. It has to be licensed for highway travel and fitted with directional lights. The electrical hookup can become a nuisance — always in the need of repair. You will also have to have your truck or sedan rigged for towing the boat. This means wires that can be connected to the trailer wires and a ball for your trailer to hook to.

Depending upon the weather, your catch can be kept on a stringer, dropped in a live well, or stored on ice. Few jon boats have live wells. A stringer is fine except in real hot weather when the surface of the water may be warm. Then it's best to attach a line and lower the fish deeper to colder water. Ideally, however, an ordinary ice chest is a better solution. I keep one in my fishing boat. It serves to keep drinks cold and at the same time preserves my catch in fine shape.

Finally, you may want to attach some rod racks to the sides of your boat. Much better having your rods secured in place when not in use than loose in the bottom where they might be stepped on.

Some bass anglers like a canoe. It's a highly versatile craft, but much better for fishing a river than a lake or pond. The modern canoe is light, easily transported on the top of an automobile, and much better for easing through rapids and shoals than a jon boat. It, however, is a little awkward to fish from, and you don't have room for the equipment you can carry in a jon boat.

Possibly you already own a canoe, or want one for purposes other than fishing. If so, by all means go that route. You will catch a lot of bass in a canoe. I have owned one for years and I've taken untold numbers of smallmouth bass, and not a few largemouths, from it. It's easier to launch where facilities are crude at the best, and easy to transport on the highway. You might consider adding a motor rack for a trolling motor or even a small outboard motor. I own a motor rack, but rarely use it. When I want to use either my electric or outboard motor I simply go with my boat which is already equipped for these conveniences.

A handy little portable boat for fishing small waters.
(Plano Molding company photo.)

I would go with drab colors instead of the bright colors on the market to day. We're talking about a fishing boat or one also used for hunting — not just for canoeing, a sport in itself.

Another option, a somewhat attractive one, is an inflatable boat or raft. Portability is a major feature here. The raft can be deflated and stored in the trunk of your automobile, but then inflated when you get to where you want to fish. Deflated, the boats are easy to transport in your hand or even in a pack. This means you can get a boat to some remote waters that are seldom fished — except from the banks. Much of the water may be beyond the reach of bank fishermen.

These boats range in length from about six feet to 12 feet or longer, and are rated as two-man boats, three-man, and on up.

They come equipped with oar locks and a pair of oars, but you might want to add a canoe paddle for working a shore line or other close handling. Except for the very small boats, most can accommodate a trolling motor or an outboard of two or three horsepower.

The stability of these inflatable boats is amazing. My wife and I once took a rafting trip down the Colorado River in an inflatable boat that carried six passengers plus the oarsman who sat near the middle of the craft and maneuvered it expertly through some of the wildest rapids in the famous river. Not once did we seem in danger of overturning, though I understand it does happen occasionally.

These inflatable boats are fairly roomy and can accommodate the anglers and their usual bass tackle. I believe we will see and hear more of this kind of boat in the future.

Several years ago a friend gave me a hard plastic boat that I've converted into a stable one-man craft for fishing small streams and ponds. It's light, easy to handle, and very stable on the water. It was originally built so that the feet could drop through an opening between the two tubes that float the angler and his tackle. I didn't like fishing with my feet in the water so I fitted a piece of plywood to cover the opening and now fish with my feet safe and dry on the little platform.

The tough little craft even has a motor mount on it and a space near the stern for a battery. I'm sure I could mount my trolling motor there with the battery just forward of it and make good progress in traveling. I haven't tried that and doubt that I will. I use the boat on small waters where the only power I need is a canoe paddle. I even shortened the handle on the paddle.

I placed a pair of hooks in the plywood, one to hold the paddle when it's not it use. I tie the paddle to a line from the plywood and let it float alongside the boat. The other hook I use to fasten my fish stringer to. I'm not sure how the manufacturer would react to what I've done to his little boat, but it meets a need for me when I want to fish small creeks or ponds.

Other possibilities include folding boats, small plastic boats that can be folded flat and carried on the roof of a small automobile. At the fishing site they are simply unfolded and launched. One I tried was a bit unsteady, so check the stability before heading out into deep water. I one I tried actually dumped me when I reached over the side for something, probably leaning too much when I did so. Such a boat is not practical for an angler who often leans over the side to free a snagged lure, remove a bass from a lure, or to place a fish on his stringer. All common movements for a bass angler.

Finally, there is the tube. I first became acquainted with this handy little boat — if you want to call it that — back in the 1960's when I was looking for something to solve a stream fishing problem. I will discuss that in the next chapter, but want to point out its possibilities as a substitute for a boat.

My old tube was nothing more than a canvas cover into which I inserted a truck inner tube and filled it with air. The inflated tube, or doughnut if you prefer, had a harness type seat which I could climb into and float or ride very comfortably. My feet were in the water, of course, but if I wanted dry feet I simply pulled on my chest waders — which I wear anyway when fishing most streams. In warm weather the angler can get his feet wet with no risk to his health. That saves the trouble of packing waders. My old bubble had a pocket for a small lure kit and loops to which I could snap a fish stringer. It was rather simple by today's standards, but a handy piece of equipment.

The bubbles, tubes, doughnuts, or whatever you prefer to call them are much more complicated today. Obviously whoever came up with the original idea had a good one. The modern ones have become very popular.

The modern name is belly boat, and they are fitted with a bevy of handy additions far superior to my old model. Typical are back supports, arm rests, up to a half dozen pockets, D-rings, and even mesh aprons to provide working space. They are relatively inexpensive ranging from approximately $50 to $150. They won't replace a boat completely and mobility is limited and slow, but they are light and easy to pack in to remote waters. Kick fins that fit on the feet are a modern accessory that the angler can wear to provide mobility.

I wouldn't be without my old doughnut, but it is actually

a poor substitute for a true boat. A small inflatable boat might be a better choice, but much is up to the individual angler and the kind of water he wants to fish. I can't think of many situations when the inflatable wouldn't get me where the belly boat would — and I wouldn't have to pack waders to keep my feet dry.

That's a quick rundown on the boat possibilities as they exist today. Tomorrow some enterprising angler may come up with something else. Bass fishing is so popular and generates so much money in the economy that it is continuously attracting new ideas.

Of the inexpensive boats available today, however, I believe the jon boat is the best choice for most situations.

Inflatable rafts are becoming increasingly popular for fishing and other water recreation.

Chapter VI
Outfitting the Wading Angler

Wading is often the most effective way to fish for bass. If you move slowly and carefully you are less likely to frighten spooky bass, and you offer a lower profile than when fishing from a boat — or even from the bank. Another advantage is that you are inclined to work the water more carefully. A drifting or moving boat often causes an angler to pass up or overlook many spots that might well hold fish. This is particularly true in stream fishing — and it is in streams that wading can be the most productive.

On the downside, wading can limit the angler in the amount

The author fishes Oregon's Umpqua River for smallmouth bass wearing chest waders. (Ginny Gooch photo.)

of water he can cover. Or more importantly the kind of water that looks good, but is beyond his reach. The wading angler is limited to the shallows near shore in most lakes and ponds.

49

Still, regardless of where you fish there is almost always going to be some good bass water that is best fished by wading. We come back to stealth and low profile which can often enhance your chances of success considerably.

Wading could easily be the next step above bank or shore fishing, and possibly this chapter should have come before the previous one on boats. It is my feeling, however, that once an angler gets into bass fishing he will want to move into some kind of boat as soon as possible. Going back to my own early bassing years, I remember how anxious I was for a boat. It was partly the romance of the move, and partly because it would give me access to so much more water, water impossible to reach from the shore — or even by wading.

I spent a lot of my fishing time in my early years on small streams, and I suspect I spent about as much time in the stream as on the banks. Wading wasn't that big a thing until I got around to approaching it on a more formal basis. I was a barefoot farm boy then and thought nothing of stepping into a stream.

But let's take a harder look. Wading presents its own unique requirements in the way of clothing as well as tactics.

Unlike the salmon or trout fisherman who fishes and wades in icy cold water, the bass fisherman is usually working warm-water streams — at least during the summer months. Those bass waters also can be cold during fall and early spring. The point is, whereas the trout or salmon angler needs hip boots or waders just about all season, the bass angler can wade wet much of the fishing year. He doesn't have to own hip boots or waders.

At the very minimum the angler getting into wading needs a pair of tennis shoes — old ones. No need to buy new shoes for wading. Dig out the oldest ones you own. I suppose ideally you could buy a pair of regular wading shoes, the kind with eyelets to let the water escape and special soles that provide good traction on slippery rocks and boulders. Most bass water, however, does not contain a lot of rocks or boulders to hamper the angler. Such bottoms are found mostly in trout streams where better foot traction is needed. And an old pair of trousers. You will want to give some attention to the trousers you wade in. Regular length pants are the best, though I often see bass anglers wading in shorts. The longer trousers provide good protection for the legs. Sure, you'll get wet, but you'll suffer fewer abrasions, cuts, and scratches if you protect your legs with trousers. There are all kinds of submerged objects to injure your legs — logs, rocks, sticks, and other objects. Protect them with those long trousers.

I was fishing with a river guide several years ago and I noticed that he wore light cotton trousers. "I get out of the boat and wade a lot," he said, "and cotton dries quickly." A worthwhile point to remember. Blue jeans are tough and provide good protection, but they dry very slowly.

I wade wet occasionally, but I'm more comfortable in chest waders. I don't like wrinkled toes that come from long hours in the water, nor do I like to live for long in wet clothing. Hip boots are fine for the smaller streams, but they limit your movement if there is much waist-deep water. In the larger streams you will find much water of that depth or even deeper. Even with waders there will be some water you can't reach. My waders are insulated because I wear them for duck hunting during some of the coldest months of the year — and for wading cold trout streams. For bass fishing, however, you don't need the insulation. Those without insulation are generally the least expensive, a thought to consider if you will fish for bass only. A regular fishing vest with as many pockets as you can get on it is a fine vehicle for carrying all of the tackle you need on a wading trip. Most vests are built with trout fishermen in mind, but they can serve the wading angler well regardless of what he fishes for. A sturdy one with roomy pockets will carry all the tackle a bass angler needs for wading a stream.

Even when clad in chest waders there will be water you can't get through. It's too deep. This bugged me for years, particularly when I was fishing down a good stream and came to a pool I couldn't fish because of the depth. To get beyond it, and downstream where I could continue fishing, I was forced to leave the stream, sometimes climb a steep bank, and often wade through briers that tore at my waders. A real problem, though it didn't keep me out of my favorite bass streams. Nothing did that.

A float tube can get you through deep pools when fishing streams.
(Ginny Gooch photo).

Then one day I was thumbing through a popular outdoor magazine and saw an advertisement touting a canvas doughnut into which you could insert an automobile inner tube. Inflate it and you had a sturdy little raft. It had a saddle-type seat which an angler could straddle and ride comfortably. Was that what I needed to get through those long deep pools I was unable to wade through? It certainly looked like the answer to my problem. As I recall, the cover sold for less than ten dollars so I clipped the advertisement, wrote a check for the proper amount, and sent it off with the next mail. My purchase arrived a few days later and I was impressed with the cover. I found a good used inner tube at the local gasoline station for two bucks and I was in business. Could hardly wait to get it on the water.

Inflated, the inner tube filled the cover nicely and it was then that I discovered a couple of pockets that would be ideal for a lure kit and other needed fishing tackle. There were also a couple of loops. I immediately recognized one as being ideal means for attaching a fish stringer. The other, I decided, would be just the thing for tying a light line, with the other end fastened to my belt. I doubt that the manufacturer had this use in mind, but I had an idea born of fishing streams, particularly small ones.

It occurred to me that while this new gadget would be ideal for getting through deep water, it would not be needed for much of my fishing. What to do with it then? Let it float along behind me! That was the answer. I would use that extra loop, tie on a light line, and fasten the other end to my belt. Even then it could serve me well, carrying my lures and other tackle in the pockets and my fish stringer on the other loop. The fish I wanted to keep would stay alive and fresh — always in the water. I wouldn't even need the fishing vest I normally wore while wading.

There was still another feature of my new wading equipment. Safety. When wading streams where there is some reasonably deep water there is always the risk of suddenly going in over your head. I'm a reasonably good swimmer. In fact I once worked as a lifeguard, but I had often considered wearing a life jacket while wading. Cumbersome, I suppose, so I never got around to it. This doughnut would eliminate that need. Since it was fastened to my belt, it would always be available if I needed it. Go in over my head and I could grab the line, pull the tube to me, and float to safety. It might be difficult to climb into, but I could at least hang onto it and kick with my feet until I got to shallow water. It's a use not often considered, but a good one.

I included a section on these bubbles, doughnuts,

tubes, or whatever you might want to call them, back in Chapter V on boats. They are now called belly boats and many are much more sopthisticated than my old tube which is now over 20 years old and still in good condition.

Incidentally, when you use the belly boat you have to make a decision as to whether you want to ride it wet or keep dry with chest waders. You can go either way. Your rear end will be resting in a couple of inches of water most of the time so if you want to keep dry you will have to wear chest waders. Hip boots, obviously, won't work here. If you opt to go in tennis or wading shoes and a pair of old trousers, accept the fact that you are going to get wet up to your waist — which might not bother you.

Some anglers use flippers on their feet for fast propulsion. They are awkward to walk in, however, and for stream fishing they are unnecessary. Since I fish downstream for bass I rely on the current to carry me through the deep water. In the absence of a good current, I simply rest my fishing rod on the tube and use my hands as oars or paddles. They work fine for short distances. I don't attempt to wade streams with long, deep pools. They are best fished by canoe or some other light craft.

I've been discussing the belly boat primarily for wading streams. Certainly it can be of value on lakes and ponds, but I would limit its use to a wading accessory in most instances. Beyond that a boat of some kind is a better choice.

I often wade to fish farm ponds, working my way slowly around the edges and normally casting ahead to work my lure back parallel to the shore. It's a good way to fish farm ponds, or any small body of water. Much better than threshing through shoreline vegetation that often blocks you from the water. Occasionally, you may encounter water too deep to wade and such a situation would block further movement. Here the belly boat following along behind you secured by a light line is the answer. Some ponds tend to drop off rapidly and you might unexpectedly find yourself in water over your head. Grab that line, pull the belly boat to you, hang on, and kick yourself to shallow water and safety.

There is no current in ponds as there is in streams and propulsion could be a problem in deep water. Usually the distance is short, however, and paddling with your hands should get you through. Or you might even use shoreline vegetation to pull yourself along — if such vegetation is available. Occasionally, I have even tied on a heavy lure that sinks rapidly, cast ahead, and let it snag on the bottom. Then I simply pull myself slowly by reeling in line. As you wade and fish and use some of the accessories that add to the pleasure, you will discover other uses for those accessories and how to tackle certain problems with them. That comes under the heading of experience. Nothing like it in fishing.

There is plenty of shallow water in big lakes, particularly the natural ones. Big reservoirs, impounded water, tend to have less shallow water, but they too have some. Wading these shallows can be highly productive, irrespective of whether you are fishing for largemouth, smallmouth, or spotted bass.

Sometimes you many uncover acres of shallow flats that can produce good fishing early and late in the day when the bass leave the deep water and move into the shallows to feed. Slow, careful wading is an ideal way to fish for these bass. Low profile, and slow movement — sometimes no movement at all. Remain quietly in one place and cover the water carefully before you move. Somewhat like still-hunting for deer. You want to get your lure in front of a bass before it sees you. These feeding bass are on the move so you can often wait for them to move into your casting range. This makes wading easier, but it requires a lot of patience. A good fisherman develops that if he doesn't already have that priceless quality.

Depending upon the lake and the part of the country in which it is located, may or may not have a rocky or boulder-studded bottom. You should determine this. It dictates to a degree how you want to fish it and also what safety precautions you want to exercise. Boulder and rocks attract fish, particularly smallmouth bass, but they can present hazards for the wading angler. One thing you particularly want to watch for is sudden drop-offs that put you in water over your head before you are aware of it. Here your belly boat, secured to your belt, is particularly important. It could save your life.

In most big lakes, even the reservoirs, there is often shallow water far from shore, out toward the middle of the lake. This water is best fished from a boat, but if you have confidence in your ability to take more fish by wading you can use a boat to reach it and then wade. Drop-offs are even more of a hazard here, however, so you want that belly boat.

Many anglers fish some very large lakes by wading and they are highly successful. Even the shallow waters of big Lake Erie, noted for its fine smallmouth bass fishing, offers this opportunity. Wave action on the larger bodies of water can be a problem for wading anglers, however, and there is really no solution to it. If the waves get too big, the best thing to do is fish from shore or call it a day and go back when the weather is more favorable.

Wading anglers are often sharing those popular shallow flats with boat anglers, so keep an eye out for them. It's matter of courtesy and also safety. You don't want to be run down by a speeding bass boat. The angler may not be aware of your presence, though that is probably not much of a possibility.

Depending upon the lake, the bottom may pitch sharply down to deep water giving you little or no wading opportunity, or it may stretch out from shore for hundreds of yards. Knowing the lake is important and you can learn much about it by reading a topographic map. A good one can be a real source of information for the wading angler.

Wading is a highly productive way to catch bass whether you are fishing a tiny inland stream or the flats of a large lake or reservoir. The wader gets in there with the fish. That's part of the attraction.

Chapter VII
The Bass Trio

The bass is actually a member of the sunfish family. Yes, the sunfish family that includes even the little bluegill and pumpkinseed among others. We won't worry about the panfish here, however, but will concentrate on the three black bass, the largemouth, smallmouth, and spotted. There are several subspecies of the three major classifications, but we won't take the space and time to discuss them. You can read about them in any number of field guides.

Of the three, the largemouth bass, *Micropterus salmoides*, is the most widespead and probably most sought after — mainly because it is so accessible to so many anglers. Smallmouth fanciers may insist their fish is a better one. If they feel that way, let it be. There is nothing objectionable about an angler enjoying and bragging about his favorite fish.

Like all of the bass, the largemouth is a grand game fish. It hits hard, fights hard, and can be taken by a variety of angling methods ranging from the kid with his cane pole and a worm to the most sophisticated fly fisherman. That wide range of angling possibilities adds to its popularity.

The fish is chunkily built. So much so that I once caught a two pounder in the St. Lawrence River that was under the minimum size limit. I don't recall what the size limit was, but my partner and I measured that fish every way we could think of but couldn't make a legal one out of it. I was fishing as a press angler in a BASS tournament. The press angler who checked in the biggest fish would win $500, and a 2-pound largemouth is a big fish in that cold northern river. In the South, however, it wouldn't raise an eyebrow.

That tells you something about the largemouth. A 4 pounder is a good fish in northern waters, but fish in the eight to 10-pound class are common in the South. The world record, a giant 22-pound, 4-ounce largemouth, was caught in Georgia back in 1932. It has been threatened several times, but remains unbroken. The lucky angler who tops that fish will earn fame and possibly even a small fortune.

The best way to distinguish the largemouth from the smallmouth and spotted bass is to check the jawbone. If it extends be-

Professional bass angler Woo Daves caught this nice largemouth bass on spinning tackle.

hind the back of the eye, it is a largemouth. The dorsal fin is so deeply notched that it appears to be completely divided. It is not so notched in the other two. It is called green bass in some waters and this gives you a hint as to its general color. Dark dots along its sides appear as a horizontal line. Otherwise, a dark back pales gradually to a white belly. In some waters the white belly is more likely to have a golden tinge — and the back may be darker. The water the fish lives in has a lot to do with its coloration. There are usually nine to 12 rows of scales on its cheeks.

Don't let those common names throw you off. Over the years and in various parts of its range, it has been called bayou bass, grass bass, green trout, lake bass, marsh bass, moss bass, Oswego bass, slough bass, and straw bass. These odd common names can provide hints regarding its appearance and habitat.

Even in its native range, the largemouth bass enjoyed

a large chunk of the North American continent. It was found from southern Canada through the Great Lakes system and down the Mississippi Valley to even Florida and Mexico. Along the Atlantic coast it was found from Maryland to Florida. The fish's original range, however, long ago lost its significance. The fish has now been widely introduced and healthy self-sustaining populations are found in every state except Alaska. It is found now in Hawaii and even in foreign countries such as South Africa. Cuba has excellent largemouth bass fishing. The bass angler is seldom far from good fishing.

The largemouth lives is such a great variety of water, from clear mountain lakes to sluggish and often murky tidal streams, that pinning down its habitat requirements is all but impossible. Ideally, however, the fish prefers warm, somewhat sluggish water, and often in water over a mud bottom. While bass love weed beds for feeding, they spend most of their time in deeper water. A good place to look for them is a drop-off to deep water near a good weed bed. It offers them a good feeding area and safety nearby in the deeper water.

Despite its popularity among anglers, the largemouth bass is a moody fish. Some days it will seemingly hit anything an angler throws in the water, but at other times you can dangle its favorite food in front of its face and it will turn and fin slowly away. "We're fishing a storm front," professional angler Woo Daves once told me when we were experiencing poor fishing on Virginia's Lake Chesdin. "That storm that just passed through turned them off, and it will be a couple of days before they are back on their feed." I'd experienced the same thing years earlier when a friend and I drove all night to reach Virginia's Back Bay to catch the dawn fishing. It was to no avail. We couldn't raise a fish. "That northeaster that blew in a couple of days ago turned them off," an old-timer back at the dock told us when we returned defeated and tired. "It will take a few calm days to get things back to normal." Largemouth bass can be caught on surface lures in only two or three feet of water but also on plastic worms at depths of 30 feet or more.

The season and time of day has a lot to do with where you find them. During the heat of summer, the bass will move into the shallows early and late in the day and at night, but the rest of the time they are out there in the deep water. Night fishing can be good for those who are willing to try it. Many anglers do not like to fish at night. It may vary to a degree by region, but the largemouth's preferred water temperature is in the 65 to 70 degrees range. And that can be part of the secret to locating the fish. Seek out its preferred temperature. This may be very deep in hot weather. Bass also move into the shallows in the spring to spawn. "They are very vulnerable during the spawning season," said one fisheries biologist who was obviously a bit concerned about the fishing pressure the fish is subjected to at that season. Some of the largest bass of the year, usually females, are taken during the spawning season.

Fishing surface lures for largemouth bass feeding in the shallows can be one of angling's greatest experiences. Toss something like a Hula Popper out there in the weeds, let it rest while the ripples fade away, and then jiggle it gently. The chances are good the weed bed will explode with action as some old mossback shatters the surface in a shower of spray and smacks that innocent lure. "It just doesn't get any better," one veteran angler told me.

While the largemouth bass enjoys wide popularity, there are those who insist the fish can't come near the spunky smallmouth, *Microperus dolomieui.* I guess I lean in that direction, but I refuse to underrate the largemouth. One thing the smallmouth has going for it is the colder water it usually lives in. It adds zest to the fish's battle with an angler. But I've also caught largemouths in smallmouth water and there is little difference between the two when they are given the same environment. Mostly it's a matter of angler preference.

You can separate the smallmouth from the largemouth by studying its jawbone. Unlike the largemouth whose jawbone extends to the rear of the eyes, the smallmouth's does not extend beyond the eyes. When you get the chance place the two fish side-by-side and the difference will become obvious. This is the best way to develop the ability to distinguish between the two fish. They are often found in the same water. The dorsal fin is not as deeply notched as in the largemouth and there are 12 or more rows of cheek scales. The smallmouth's eyes are red whereas the largemouths are much darker colored.

Experienced bass fisherman, however, do not have to go to this kind of trouble to distinguish between the two fish. They can just about tell what they have on their lines by the fish's fight. The smallmouth's runs are faster, more spirited than the slower runs and slugging fight of the largemouth. And instead of the closely spaced spots which form a horizontal line along the flanks of the largemouth, The smallmouth's flanks are marked with vertical bars. The fish is more likely to have a bronzed coloring than the green tint of the largemouth.

Author with a nice smallmouth bass caught on spinning tackle. (Ginny Gooch photo.)

In fact a favorite common name for the smallmouth is bronzeback.

Over the years the smallmouth has also collected a batch of common names. Among them are Achigan, black bass, black perch, bronzeback, brown bass, gold bass, little bass, redeye, Swago bass, and tiger bass. Such common names give hints to the nature of the fish, redeye — for example — because of its red eyes. Bronzeback, brown bass, and redeye are the most popular.

Generally, the smallmouth is a smaller fish than the largemouth. The average fish will probably run 1 1/2 to 2-pounds, and a 4 pounder is a good fish is most waters. The smallmouth's size does not vary much from one region to another, but the world record came from Tennessee in 1955. That fish, at 11 pounds, 15 ounces, was approximately half the weight of the world record largemouth. Remember that and you will be in the ball park when someone asks you the sizes of the world record largemouth and small-mouth bass. The original range of the smallmouth bass didn't nearly approach that of the largemouth. Initially it was found primarily in the Ohio River drainage system and in both the Canadian and American drainage systems of the Great Lakes. But that original range has long since become insignificant. The fish have been introduced to new waters, lakes and river, from southern Canada south to Alabama, and from the Atlantic Coast to the Pacific. There is excellent smallmouth fishing in such waters as the Umpqua River in Oregon, the James and Potomac rivers systems in the East and throughout the Northeast. There is excellent fishing in states such as California, Oklahoma, and Texas — far from the original range of the scrappy fish. Both private and public interests have been instrumental in spreading this fine game fish across America.

The smallmouth bass is a bit more finicky in accepting suitable water than is the largemouth. True, the two fish are often found in the same waters, but it is usually a case of the largemouth accepting good smallmouth water. Seldom the reverse. This common water may be either a lake or a stream, but possibly more often a cold lake.

Clear water is a must for the smallmouth. It may be either a lake or a stream, but it must be clear. The stream must be a flowing one. The best offer plenty of rapids and riffles, plus boulders, rocks, and rocky cliffs. I fish streams for smallmouths a lot, and the water that first catches my eye is a rocky shoreline with rich weed beds bordering it. The fish is rarely present in sluggish water. The water must also be cold, but not as cold as that found in good trout streams. It is a fact, however, that brown trout and smallmouth bass sometimes share a stream. The fish's preferred water temperature is in the 65 to 67 degrees range.

While lake smallmouths tend to share the largemouth's mood which turns it off with weather changes, I do not believe the river fish is as much affected by the weather. The biggest weather problem the river smallmouth angler has is muddy and swollen water following a heavy rain. Rain upstream that you may not even be aware of can eventually send those muddy waters to your favorite stretch of a stream. This hampers the angler mostly because the visibility is so limited in the off-color water the fish can't see a lure.

The smallmouth also likes to feed in the shallows early and late in the day. Night fishing is also good, but fishing streams at night can be risky in strange waters. The best smallmouth waters are characterized by underwater boulders, sudden drop-offs, and other features which make good smallmouth fishing, but present dangers for the wading angler. Such water is best fished during the daylight hours. Fishing lakes for smallmouths is much like fishing for largemouth bass. It's a safer place for night fishing.

Smallmouth bass love fast water, probably because it often holds crayfish, minnows, and other food. Those fast stretches are usually also shallow, and even the lunkers move into them early and late in the day. As the day progresses, however, the big fish move back into deep water and you have to look for them there. The smaller bass will remain in the riffles and runs just about throughout the day.

The spotted bass, *Micropterus pinctulatus*, is the least known of the three black bass because of its more limited range. The fish was first discovered in Kentucky and for that reason it is sometimes called Kentucky bass. It is built along the lines of the other two basses, chunky or stubby. It seems to lean toward the smallmouth in personality, but it has many of the markings of the large-

Successful lady angler with a nice spotted bass. (Photo by Bill Vanderford.)

mouth. Generally smaller in size than the largemouth and smallmouth, an Alabama fish holds the world record. It was caught back in 1978 and weighed 8 pounds, 15 ounces. It has several rows of distinct spots running horizontally along its flanks, but can be hard to identify. It is easily confused with the largemouth, but its mouth will help here. The point of its jaw is a bit further back than that of the smallmouth, but forward of that of the largemouth. The dorsal fin is not as deeply notched as that of the largemouth and it usually has 12 or more rows of cheek scales.

The fish was originally found from southern Ohio and West Virginia to southern Illinois, Kansas, Oklahoma, eastern Texas, and east to Alabama, western Georgia, Virginia and the Tennessee River drainage. That range has been extended somewhat by stocking, but not nearly to the

64

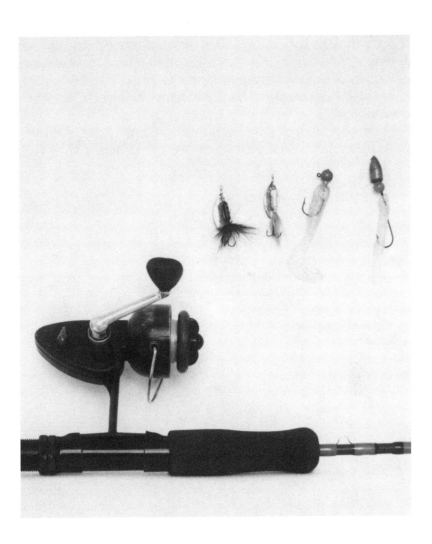

Spinning lures that will take spotted bass.

extent of that of the other two black bass.

It seems willing to accept more sluggish waters in the North probably because they are colder. In the South it likes cooler streams with gravel and sand bottoms.

In feeding it resembles the habits of the smallmouth, but it does not prefer water as cold as that the smallmouth thrives in. It leans more toward rocks and boulders than it does toward the weeds loved by the largemouth. It also seems to prefer moving water, but it is found in a number of lakes, a noteworthy one being Georgia's Lake Lanier. Even there it was in the main river before it was impounded.

I caught my first spotted bass in a clear spring-fed river in southern Kansas, and have been impressed with this little bass from the first. I could have jumped across that little Kansas River.

The basses three. That's what this book is all about.

Chapter VIII
Bass Fishing Basics

The bass is a structure-oriented fish. It matters not whether you are fishing for a largemouth, smallmouth or spotted bass, you are most likely to find it close to some kind of cover. And it matters not whether you are fishing a canal or ditch, lake, pond, river, small stream, or some other kind of bass water. Look for bass near structure as modern bass anglers call cover.

That structure can take many forms. Smallmouth bass love rocky cover — boulders, cliffs, or rocks. Largemouth and spotted bass like docks, duck blinds, inundated brush piles, weed beds, or any other such structure that offers a little shade from the sun, cover from predators, or an ambush spot for prey. Spotted bass, like the smallmouth, are attracted to rocks more than largemouth are. Largemouth bass like drop-offs, especially those near shallows where they can make a fast escape to deep water if necessary. About the only limit on possible cover is the imagination. Just about any foreign matter that breaks up open water should be checked out. In farm ponds, for example, they often relate to the drainage pipe.

This doesn't mean you won't find bass in open water. You will, particularly during feeding sprees.

All of the black bass like weed beds, but the largemouth is probably drawn to them the most. I never, however, pass up a good weed bed regardless of what kind of bass I'm fishing for.

Largemouths, particularly those in the deep reservoirs, seek deep water during the heat of summer. Some may sink as much as 30 feet to locate the temperatures they prefer. In shallow waters bass often seek the shade of boat docks, overhanging trees, and other shade from the sun. They move into the shallows mostly at night, but may also be found there early and late in the day — or after the sun loses some of its sting.

As a general rule, river bass seem to accept shallow water better than do those of the lakes. One reason is that the current, moving waters, creates more oxygen in the streams.

For most of the year, but particularly in the summer months, the best bass fishing occurs at night — after the sun has left the water and darkness creeps over the land. The next best time to fish for bass is at dawn and a short time thereafter, depending upon how hot the weather is, or at dusk. If you plan to devote an entire day to bass fishing, then look for water that is protected from the sun — or fish deep during the midday hours.

Another advantage of fishing at night is the fact that the angler is less visible to the bass — even in shallow water. Night is an excellent time to fish the shallows. The bass are more likely to be there then and the angler is less conspicuous. To a lesser degree this is also true at dawn or dusk, at least before and after the sun has left the water. Dawn comes early during the summer months, and it is then that many bass anglers are drawn early to their favorite waters. Let's assume you have an hour's drive to reach your bass water, and you'll probably want to eat breakfast before you leave — or en route. That probably means setting your alarm for 3 a.m. — and the risk of waking up the entire household. Still, dawn fishing can be good, and it is particularly attractive during those warm months when the bass visit the shallows only at night or dawn and dusk. If the fishing water is not too far away, I get up, go fishing, and get home in time for a normal breakfast. It can be worth the effort. When planning a dawn fishing trip, I like to be on the water at first light -- long before the sun hits the water.

Both dawn and dusk, incidentally, plus night are ideal times to fish topwater lures. A big old bass smacking a topwater lure under the cover of darkness can be unnerv-

Dawn and dusk can be prime fishing times.

ing. You feel and hear, but don't see the strike.

Dusk fishing can be easier. No need to lose sleep. On long summer evenings you can eat dinner at home and then get in a couple of hours of fishing before dark. Or if you prefer, you can pack a picnic and eat on the water. Over the years, however, it has been my experience that those early morning hours are more productive.

Night fishing requires a certain amount of preparation prior to darkness when visibility is reduced substantially. You will need a light of some kind, but it should not be so bright as to cast too strong a beam. You will need it for changing lures, releasing fish, and other fishing tasks. It's also a good idea to arrange your tackle before darkness so you will know where it is. That way you won't be fumbling around in the dark attempting to locate something you have an immediate need for.

Dawn, dusk, and night offer other advantages, the absence of boaters, for example, and particularly water skiers. And you can leave your Sun Block at home. On the other hand mosquitos can be a problem on some waters, particularly if you happen to be working a shoreline. You'll need night lights on your boat — even if fishing only to dusk but making the run back to the dock as darkness gathers. Fishing a stream after dark can be particularly dangerous if you have to run rapids on a strange river. I really can't recommend fishing a strange river after dark. Make a daytime trip first and become familiar with it. To a degree this also holds for lakes. The more you know about them, the more successful you will be when fishing lakes at night.

Tidal streams present a different problem and require a different approach. The tide, not the sun or the time of day, guides the successful bass angler. Tides offer moving water, and the fishing is best on moving water. It slows noticeably when the water stops moving. That occurs at both high and low tides — or flood and ebb tides. A fellow bass angler introduced me to fishing tidal rivers a number of years ago. We caught an incoming tide and enjoyed fast fishing until it hit the high point and then we might as well have called it a day. Nothing moved, the water or the bass. We took time for a leisurely lunch, and when we returned to our boat, the tide was beginning to move out and the fish began hitting again.

A set of tide charts can be one of the tidal river bass anglers most valuable tools. They are also published in many newspapers and also in saltwater fishing magazines.

Tidal rivers offer an interesting kind of bass fishing, something that no other bass water offers. We will discuss this in more detail in the chapter on fishing rivers.

The weather is something the bass angler has no control over, but he can use it in planning his outings so he will be on the water at the very best times. Most anglers are familiar with the Solunar Tables which indicate the prime hunting and fishing periods each month. Some anglers swear by them, but others ignore them. Most of us fish when we can work it into our schedules. It's our recreation and just getting out there on the water and relaxing is much of what it is all about. Viewed in that light the time of day, month, or year is of little consequence. There are few hours, days, months, or seasons when you can't catch at least a few bass.

For the very best fishing, however, it is important to take the weather into consideration. Bass seldom hit well immediately after a storm has blown through. This is more true of largemouth bass than of spotted or smallmouths. It usually takes a couple of days for the fish to get back to their normal feeding patterns. In the meantime you will still catch some fish, but your chances are reduced significantly. That storm can be a hurricane, thunderstorm, tornado, or just a couple of days of strong wind out of the northeast. So keep that in mind when you are planning a trip.

Some of my most memorable fishing trips have come when it was raining — not a downpour, but a steady rain or even better a drizzle rain. While you will catch some fish during such weather you will also suffer some discomfort. The thing you have to decide is whether or not the fishing is worth it. Put on modern rain clothing and you can keep reasonably dry.

You can also catch bass during a thunderstorm, but the fishing will drop off soon after the storm has passed. But there is a safety factor to be considered here. A lake, and to a less degree a river, can be an extremely dangerous place during a thunderstorm. Lightning is a part of such weather and it can be the major hazard. Lightning is drawn to the highest points on the land or water. On land it is often a lone tree in an open field, but on water it is more likely to be a boat out there in the storm. You don't want to be in that boat.

Other hazards include high winds which can overturn or swamp your boat. And on a stream, particularly a small one which rises quickly, there is always the risk of flash floods.

Keeping abreast of the weather forecasts can mean better fishing and safer fishing.

Bass fishing can be an all-year activity. Sure the fish's metabolism slows down in cold weather, but it continues to feed. It's just that it is less active and requires less food. There are two times, or seasons if you prefer, that you have

A successful winter bass angler.

to go deep for bass. One is the heat of summer and the other the coldest months of the year. In much of the best bass fishing country the hot months are late June, July, August, and early September. The coldest months are late December, January, February, and early March. Because the fish are deep then, these can be the least productive months to fish — or the bass are more difficult for the novice angler to locate and catch.

The usual approach to summer fish that are deep in some lake or big river is to work the bottom with plastic worms or grubs. This means going deep, sometimes as much as 30 feet. It's also a good time to fish deep-running crankbaits, those with long lips that drive the lure deep.

The other two seasons, basically the spring and fall months, are the best fishing months. In the spring the bass are in the shallows spawning and very vulnerable. It's a good time to fish the shoreline with buzzbaits, spinnerbaits, shallow-running crankbaits, or topwater lures.

In the fall the fish move back into the shallows, go on

To avoid injury to a bass you plan to release grasp it by the lips.

72

feeding sprees, and store up energy for the winter. They are accessible and ready to hit. Those same lures that produced earlier during the spawning season will put bass on the stringer or in the live well in the fall also. Or maybe you just want to catch the fish and then release them. If you do, handle them with care.

Seasons vary somewhat depending upon the part of the country you call home, but this is the general pattern, and it can be altered to a particular region. In the North, for example, ice can be a problem. Both lakes and streams freeze over and bass anglers have to join the frostbite crew and chop a hole in the ice to reach the water. I've caught a few bass through the ice, but it's an entirely different ball game. The other thing to consider is that in a few states the bass fishing season is closed during the spawning period. So you will have to work around that.

Good knots are basic to fishing. You want knots that are easy to tie, but ones that are going to hold up under the stress of casting lures or bait and fighting fish. Your fishing tackle is subjected to almost continuous pressure of one kind or another during a long period of fishing. Modern tackle, rods, reels, and lines are built to withstand heavy use, but unless you can tie strong knots you will lose both fish and lures — unnecessarily.

Every knot you tie weakens your line to a degree, but some knots are more likely to do so than others. Over the years I've used a pair of knots that seem to fill all of my fishing needs.

The one I use most is the improved clinch knot. Some knot experts insist others are better, but this old favorite has served me well. It's the one I use most frequently when the hook or lure has a small eye. To tie it I run the end of my line or leader through the hook, double it back and wrap it back on itself a half dozen times. I then run the end through the loop formed where I double it back. Snugged tightly, this is a good knot. I prefer, however, the improved clinch knot. To tie it you simply run the end of your line through the loop a second time before snugging it up. Snugging the knot tightly is very important to assure that it will hold.

The palomar is another popular knot, but its use is limited to hooks or lures with fairly large eyes. To tie it you double the end of your line back on itself and run the doubled strands through the eye. That's why it is difficult to tie when the eye is small. Pull the double line through far enough to tie an overhand knot in the double part of the line. This leaves a loop in the end of the line, and through this you pull the hook and then snug the knot tightly. Again we have a strong knot for bass fishing. Take your choice. Some anglers prefer the improved clinch knot while others prefer the palomar. Ideally, you should practice tying your favorite one until you can do it with your eyes closed — handy for night fishing.

That's bass fishing basics as I see it. I usually start the bass season in March as the fish move into the shallows to spawn. The bass is highly vulnerable then and you are likely to catch some big females. If so, handle them carefully and let them go. That move helps insure the future of bass fishing.

I work the shoreline initially, fishing crankbaits, spinnerbaits, and occasionally even plastic worms. If a fish rolls at your spinnerbait, but does not take it, switch to a juicy-looking plastic worm and cast it back to the same water. You just might take that bass that did no more than make a pass at your crankbait or spinnerbait. Work those lures fairly rapidly — and steadily. Late in the spring when the spawn is over, but the fish are still in the shallows, I like to toss topwater or surface lures.

When hot weather comes on, I switch to plastic worms mostly and work them deep and reasonably slow. I will quickly confess, however, that this is not my favorite method of bass fishing. I'm more inclined to find a good river or stream and switch my bassin' efforts to that until cool weather brings the fish back into the shallows. Then it's topwater lures as much as possible. During the winter months, I'm too busy hunting to try to catch sluggish bass.

Chapter IX
The Cast and the Strike

It was steaming hot that August morning on the James River. Even the dawn had broken warm and humid, despite the fact that there is always a breath of air on a fast-flowing river. The river currents seem to keep a little air stirring even when the countryside is deadly still and the air hangs heavy.

Despite the oppressive heat, this was bass fishing weather and life on the river was at least bearable. What avid bass angler won't accept a little discomfort for some good fishing?

But the bass had quit hitting.

There had been a brief flurry of activity at dawn — promising. But then the sun had peeked over the horizon to bath the river in its steaming rays. As it did so the action had ceased as suddenly as if someone had inadvertently thrown a switch.

Sure, we continued to fish. Isn't that always true when good fishing suddenly becomes poor? You don't quit immediately. Typically, we kept trying, making cast after cast, and trying all kinds of water and a variety of lures. But to no avail. Would we go home with the few bass we had caught at dawn and soon thereafter?

"They're probably back in the shade of that overhanging vegetation along the shore," suggested my partner from the stern of the canoe. "They'll be hard to catch there."

"Let's move in close and give it a try," I suggested.

Fishing that shoreline wouldn't be easy. No way you could get a lure beneath that vegetation with a conventional cast.

"Hold it right there and let me try a side cast," I said

when we were within approximately 30 feet of the tree-lined bank.

I reeled my tiny surface lure to within about six inches of the tip of my light spinning rod, leaned forward over the bow of the canoe, and keeping the rod tip close to the surface of the water, shot the lure toward an opening in the bank cover. My first cast was off, but fortunately I was able to retrieve the lure from a low branch of a willow. The second try was more successful and the lure scooted beneath the overhanging willow limbs and splashed lightly down within inches of the almost hidden river bank.

"Pure luck," I mumbled to myself.

I flicked the lure once and the water boiled!

I could feel the slashing strike all the way to my elbow. The fish leaped immediately, and then dove for the bottom, but the brisk battle ended quickly as I worked a nice 12-inch smallmouth bass to the canoe.

Had I not been reasonably proficient with the side cast, our long-planned fishing trip on the James River would have ended early that day. Those bass had deserted the open river and the bright rays of the sun early that late summer morning for the shady comfort of the bank vegetation. And casting to the edge of the cover was not going to budge them. We had to get our lures well back under the cover to interest them.

The side cast is one of several more or less unorthodox spinning casts that will help the angler catch bass under difficult circumstances. Most are not too difficult to master. They won't win casting tournaments, but they will put fish in the live well or on the stringer when the conventional overhand cast can produce little more than healthy exercise. We are talking primarily about spinning tackle here, but the bait-casting angler will also find use for it, and I've even used it when fly fishing.

But before we go further let's pause and take a quick look at the conventional overhand cast, the one the beginning angler should master first. It's fairly simple.

Pick up your rod in your casting hand — right or left — reel the lure within approximately six inches of the tip of the

The overhand cast is the norm for spinning, but the forward motion of the rod should be halted at 11 o'clock.

rod and grasp the line with the index finger of your casting hand. Press the index finger with the line against the rod handle. Point the tip of the rod toward the target, the spot where you want to place your lure, and bring the tip of the rod up sharply to the one o'clock position. This places the tip of the rod and the lure slightly behind you. Now bring the rod sharply forward releasing the line from beneath the index finger as you do. Done correctly this should shoot the lure toward your target on the water. A few hours of practice and you will have this down to the point you are comfortable with it. All other casts, including the side cast already discussed, are deviations of the conventional over-hand cast.

Here are a couple of things to remember. A common mistake is to drop the rod beyond the one o'clock position on the back cast. When you do this you tend to release the line on the upward swing and this shoots the lure high in the air — unfortunately often over a tree branch of some other elevated structure that might rob you of a good lure.

The length of line left dangling at the end of the rod is also a factor. Or in other words the amount of line between the tip of the rod and the lure. Roughly six inches of line is the usual recommendation, but you can control your casts to a degree by altering this. If you are seeking better accuracy and less distance reduce the amount, but if you want to achieve distance at the expense of accuracy, lengthen the distance between the rod tip and the lure.

The more you cast and fish, or simply practice cast in your back yard, the more comfortable you will become with the little adjustments you can make to increase you casting efficiency — and this translates into more successful fishing and more fighting bass out there on the end of your line. That's the ultimate goal of all of your casting efforts.

A landing net is the safest way to land a bass.

The already discussed side cast is simply a modification of the overhand cast, except that instead of bringing the rod tip up vertically to the one o'clock position before snapping it forward, you bring it back horizontally with the tip close to the surface of the water. Boat as well as wading anglers can use it — primarily to get their lures well back beneath overhanging vegetation.

But it has other uses.

I recall a brisk day on big Buggs Island Lake in Virginia when a sharp breeze had anglers holding onto their hats and bundled against the occasional gusts of icy air. But it was March and the largemouth bass were stirring, searching the shallows for spawning areas, and hitting crank and spinnerbaits tossed into the willows and worked down the points.

This was open-water fishing at its best. Under ordinary circumstances, the conventional overhand cast would have allowed pinpoint accuracy, but the wind was a factor. The spinners of a spinnerbait sailing shoreward at 10 to 15 feet above the surface were spinning madly long before the lure plunked down. And caught broadside in a gust of wind, a fat crankbait would be several feet off course before it hit the water. Accuracy was all but impossible.

We solved that problem, however, by resorting to side casts that sent our lures skimming just above the surface. In other words we cheated the wind. We couldn't avoid it completely, but we enjoyed much better control with our lures a couple of feet above the surface instead of way up there in the constant gusts.

The major problem with side casts is the lack of accuracy. Accuracy can be hard to achieve, but back-yard practice will help. Accuracy is a major advantage of the overhand cast. The angler can point his rod tip at the target, bring the tip up and back and snap it forward — right on target. This is more difficult with the side cast.

So far I've touched on the side cast delivered horizontally, but just about any deviation from the vertical overhand cast fits the description. For example, suppose you

Anglers fishing topwater baits tend to strike too quickly. They should wait until they feel the fish, otherwise they may take the lure away from the bass.

are fishing a stream and are concerned about a long tree branch that extends out over the water and in the antici-pated path of your lure. Or maybe there is a low-swinging utility line that crosses the stream. An overhand cast might send your lure above the limb or line. Depending upon the height of the limb or line, you can avoid it by resorting to a side cast somewhere between the vertical overhand position and the horizontal one.

Again, you'll probably lose some accuracy unless you have practiced enough to handle it, but you will avoid hanging a lure up there where you can't retrieve it. Lures are expensive, and you will lose enough in normal fishing situations without having sloppy casting claim them.

Master the side cast and it will solve all kinds of practical fishing problems — even it won't win casting tournaments.

A back cast is still another variation of the side cast. It is useful in cramped quarters. Let's go back to that day on the James River in Virginia, a fine smallmouth bass river. My partner in the stern of the canoe would have experienced problems with the side cast as we have so far described it. Facing into the canoe he would have found it difficult to get his spinning rod down to the horizontal position where he could deliver a good cast. Add the fact that had he gotten off an errant cast he might have hit me up there in the other end of the canoe. He solved it with a back cast. Turning slightly to face the shoreline, he brought his casting hand across his chest to a point near his opposite shoulder and made his cast by swinging his casting hand away from his chest. This cast resembles the back stroke in tennis. Handy in tight spots such as this.

The back cast offers solutions to numerous fishing situations. I've used it many times on the small streams where you can often find seldom-fished bass waters. The combination of brush-lined shores and gin-clear waters with spooky fish calls for innovations.

I recall one situation when I had worked my way slowly upstream and came upon a likely pool. I was using the branches of a tree on the right side of the stream — facing upstream — for concealment. There was no way I could make an overhand cast, and positioned as I was tightly against the bank, I couldn't resort to my usual side cast. If I had moved away from the bank to get casting room, I would have spooked every bass in the pool. The solution? A back cast — and with it I took a scrappy 15-inch spotted bass on my ultralight spinning tackle.

Some anglers speak of the bow-and-arrow cast to get a lure into tight quarters. It might have worked in the stream situation described above, but I have enjoyed limited success with this cast. Haven't really practiced it enough to put it into practical fishing situations.

To accomplish this cast you simply point the rod tip toward the spot you want your lure to land, grab the lure by the rearmost hook, pull back, bending the rod as you would a bow to shoot an arrow, and release it when you feel you have developed enough power to shoot the lure to the spot on the water where you feel it will interest a lurking or roaming bass. A word of caution. Make sure you grasp the lure to the rear of all hooks on the lure, otherwise you might drive one into your hand — a good way to end a promising fishing trip early.

Anyone who has ever fished with the age-old cane pole — and who hasn't — is familiar with the way you swing the baited hook back and forth until you get enough momentum to drop it just where you expect the big bass to be waiting. This is the principle employed in the underhand cast. It's another spinning cast, a practical deviation, that will catch bass.

The difference is that you have the fixed-spool spinning reel to hold the line until you are ready to release it — just as you do in the conventional overhand cast.

Modern bass anglers call this flipping. They use it to make short casts and keep their lures in productive water longer. A long overhand cast means that on the retrieve you must run the lure through often unproductive water before you get it back for another cast. Flipping eliminates that time in the unproductive water.

The underhand cast can also be used in tight quarters to make short casts to hard-to-reach water, water where none of the other spinning casts could be used. It's a good one to perfect if you plan to fish small streams a lot.

These are the major unorthodox spinning casts that will catch fish when the conventional overhand cast cannot be used effectively. By all means stick with the overhand cast if possible, but don't pass up good fishing water because you can't use that cast. Dig into you bag of bass-fishing tricks and pull out one of these casts.

The ones I have described are really just a beginning. The innovative angler can come up with all kinds of combinations once he has mastered the basics of casting.

These innovations allow him to get the most good out of his versatile spinning tackle. Join this school of anglers and catch more bass.

Good casting and the proper manipulation of the lure will get you strikes. Then you have another problem — setting the hook properly and keeping it set until you can land the fish.

Setting the hook. That's the key to landing a fish once it strikes. There are a pair of schools of thought on the subject. My approach, possibly one born of habit as a youngster, is to set the hook with a sharp flick of my wrist. The object, of course, is to drive the hook or hooks deep into the fish's jaw so it won't come loose too easily. Bass are noted for leaping, shaking their heads, and throwing a poorly set hook. That's what you want to avoid, and I feel you need to drive that hook only an inch or two at the most, usually not that much. And I feel a strong upward flick of the wrist should do it.

Many of the professional anglers, those who make a living fishing major bass tournaments, think otherwise. They like to get their arms into it, even their bodies. They hit hard — from the waist up you might say. They leave no doubt about the bass being soundly hooked. So that's how you set the hook. Take your choice.

Another problem is deciding when to set the hook. On most artificial lures you strike and attempt to set the hook immediately upon feeling the fish. Anxious anglers sometimes strike too quickly on surface strikes, in effect taking the lure away from the bass before it gets in his mouth. I'm sure I have been guilty of that. You strike when the see the water boil or the bass breaks the water — and too quickly. Wait until you feel the fish before striking.

An exception comes when you use natural baits such as minnows or worms. There I like to give the fish time. A bass often grabs a natural bait and makes off with it before taking it solidly in his mouth. Strike too quickly and you will pull the bait away or yank the hook free of the bait. The same is true of plastic worms. I like to give the bass time to take the worm in his mouth. The bass hits and handles a soft plastic lure much as it does natural bait.

Mastering the cast and strike is part of becoming an experienced bass angler.

Rick Clunn plays this bass carefully and will probably land it by grabbing it by the lip.

Chapter X
Care of the Catch

A surprisingly large number of anglers do not eat the bass they put so much time and effort into outwitting. Many insist they do not like fish. Others say they are interested only in the challenges and fun of fishing, and so release all of the bass they catch. Catch-and-release fishing is a bass angling buzzword today, a slogan for many bass fishing clubs. It's a worthy move on hard-fished waters where the pressure could be harmful to the resource.

By handling this bass by the lip the angler can release it without harm if he desires.

Tom Rodgers will release this smallmouth which he holds by the lips.

For some the chore of cleaning the fish is the real block. And transporting fish for many miles in hot weather does present problems which many anglers do not want to cope with.

For the bass, which must be sustained for the most part by natural reproduction — a fish that doesn't lend itself to mass put-and-take fishing as does the rainbow trout nor to prolific breeding as does the bluegill or crappie — the release of all fish caught is to be commended. For the majority of anglers, however, the fish-for-fun concept does not completely satisfy the angling appetite. These fine sportsmen are not to be condemned as meat fishermen. Taking home a good catch is part of the pleasure of fishing, the culmination of their many hours of study of angling techniques, bass habits, and all of the elements that go into a successful fishing trip. Catching a limit may be unimportant, but a handsome catch to show the family and neighbors is proof of their angling prowess. And not to be overlooked is fact that fish taken from clean waters are a healthy addition to the average American diet. The flesh of freshwater fish is high in proteins, but low in calories and fat. Bass grade out well in such tests, but more popular table fish such as crappie, yellow perch, and walleye have an edge in that respect. Bass too can contribute to a healthy diet, however, and it is for these anglers that this chapter is written.

Care for the catch begins as the threshing bass is being removed from the hook or lure. If the fish is to be kept alive — either in a live well or on a stringer — the careful removal of the hook is critical, otherwise the bass may die quickly. In cold weather, particularly, a bass is a durable fish.

A hook disgorger or a pair of long-nosed pliers are just about a necessity for the bass angler. They enable him to remove hooks or lures with a minimum of damage to the fish. The bass should be handled carefully. It is one of a few fish that can be lipped — grasped by the lower lip — and handled with ease. This seems to temporarily paralyze the bass. Don't bounce the bass off the deck of a boat or slam it against the gunwales — and don't stick a finger in the gills. This is almost certain death for a bass.

Bass kept on a stringer are usually fastened to the side of the boat, trailed from the belt of a wading angler, or fastened to a tree or stake if the angler is fishing from shore. The fish are allowed to trail in the water where they can be kept alive for an extended time — providing they are strung through both lips. They can be strung through the gills if they will remain on the stringer for a brief duration and keeping them alive is unnecessary. It should be remembered, however, that they will quickly drown if strung through the gills.

Stringered fish should be kept in cold water, particularly on a warm day if you are fishing from a boat. The surface water is likely to be very warm for several feet down, and the fish will not live long in such water regardless of how they are strung. Many bass fishermen solve this problem by attaching a light rope or small chain as an extension to their normally short stringers, and lowering their catch to deeper and cooler water. This method is not recommended for water that is filled with aquatic vegetation or other obstructions.

When moving from one spot to another it is best to bring the fish aboard and cover them with a wet burlap if necessary. Left in the water, they not only impede the progress of the boat, but they may be drowned or torn off of the stringer.

The stream angler does not have the same problem, as the flowing water is likely to be cooler and filled with life-giving oxygen.

Some boats are equipped with live wells, usually a compartment in the middle of the boat through which the lake or river water circulates. In cool weather this is an excellent way to keep fish alive, though it is not recommended when the surface water is warm or hot.

One advantage of keeping fish alive is the last-minute choice it gives the angler as to whether he wants to release the bass or take all or some of them home. If all of his catch is alive at the end of the trip, he can select those he wants to keep for the table and release the rest for another day or another angler. It relieves him of the dilemma the big-game hunter so often finds himself in. Is this rack worth taking — or will I get a better chance? The bass angler who uses a live well or a deep stringer does not have to decide at the moment whether he wants to keep the fish he has just caught. He can wait until the day is over and then select his trophies, releasing the rest.

A final word on stringers. Those with snaps for individual fish are by far the best. They space the fish properly on the stringer and thus prevent their jamming down, one on top of the other as they are prone to do on a rope stringer. Most snap stringers are made of wire and have the disadvantage of being noisy. However, some plastic models, now on the market, are durable, quiet to use, and do not rust. Also available are models on which the snaps slide up and down the stringer. These permit the angler to add a fish to the stringer without having to remove the rest of his catch from the water.

Ideally, fish should be killed as soon as they are caught, the gills and viscera removed, and the fish placed on ice. The same practice is good for wild game that the hunter bags. Removal of the blood from around the backbone is of particular importance. Since bass are usually not caught in remote wilderness areas of the United States and Canada, ice is usually readily available.

Modern plastic ice chests facilitate the use of ice. They are light, and come in a wide selection of sizes and styles. The better ones are equipped with a drain so that the excess water will run off as it melts. This is an important feature, for the fish should be kept dry as well as cold. Some ice chests have trays or ice compartments which keep the ice separated from the contents of the cooler, or keep the contents above the water which accumulates as the ice melts.

Although many anglers simply drop their freshly caught fish on the ice, it is far best to remove the gills and viscera before doing so. If this is impractical, then the fish should at least be killed before being deposited in the ice chest. A sharp rap on the head will kill a bass in short order. Any blunt instrument will do the job, though many professional fishing guides carry a billy for this purpose.

If room permits, the bass should be kept separated by chunks of ice. And while it may be purely psychological, I like to place the fish directly on the ice. A fully colored bass stretching the length of the chest and partially imbedded in the ice presents an interesting picture, the kind that fishing tackle people use to sell their products. Some fishermen prefer to place their fish in plastic bags — particularly for a long trip home.

The ice chest between these anglers is a fine place to keep their catch for table use.

If the trip home is to be a long one, the ice chest should be covered with wet burlap and placed in the car where the sun will not hit. Covering the chest with coats or other such protection also helps. It is also a good idea to cool the chest thoroughly before filling it with ice.

Drainage of the chest while on the road can create a problem, but a good way to solve it is to slip a small hose over the chest drain pipe, and run it out of the car — through a spare tire well, for example.

Properly cooled and located, and drained en route, a chest of ice will last a long time, even on a highway trip in hot weather. The size and type of chest and the temperature have a lot to do with it, of course, but replenishing the ice once daily will suffice in most cases.

For the wading angler the use of an ice chest is, of course, limited to the road trip home. On the lake or stream he must use a creel or stringer. If the bass are not too large, as is often the case with stream bass, then the angler can steal a page from the trout angler's book and creel his bass in damp leaves, ferns, grass, or moss. For the best results the fish should not be permitted to touch each other. Here again the bass should be killed as soon as it is caught and the gills and viscera removed. Bass carried in this manner should arrive home in good condition.

The angler working from the bank of a stream or the shore of a lake has a choice — creel, ice chest, or stringer. If possible he should use the ice chest. He can likely locate a cool, shady spot where the chest will fare much better than it will in a boat.

Some anglers like fish bags or burlap sacks. These can be fastened to the side of the boat or tied to a belt around the angler's waist. The fish are placed in the bag alive, and if the weather and water are cool, they will live for a long time.

The sooner a fish is cooked after being taken from the water, the better it will taste. That's one reason shore lunches are so tasty. Ideally, a bass should be battled to a standstill, removed from the lure, killed, cleaned and flopped immediately into a hot skillet. This, of course, is not always possible.

Still, the best bet is to plan an early fish meal, and cook the fish fresh from the ice chest. There is actually no off season when it comes to fishing for bass, and if the family wants a delicious fish fry during the winter, why not hie off to the nearest bass water and bring home a fresh catch. I've even taken bass through the ice in January, but in much of America you can find open water through the winter.

But there will be times when it's desirable to store at

If a stringer is used to keep bass the fish should be strung through both lips. They will drown if strung through the gills.

least part of the catch. This brings up the proper manner of preparing fish the home freezer. There's a certain fascination about freezing fish and game for later use that appeals to many outdoorsmen. Most modern food markets carry a variety of freezing containers — plastic bags, wax-coated cartons, binding tape, and wrapping wire. It's mostly a matter of personal preference as to what type to use. The only objection I have to plastic bags is that they sometimes get pierced, inviting air to get to the fish and cause freezer burn.

Preparing the bass for the freezer amounts to no more than cleaning them as if they were to go immediately to the frying pan. They can be filleted, steaked, or frozen whole. Some anglers like to place whole bass, if they are small, or fillets in empty milk cartoons and fill the carton with water before freezing. This in effect freezes the fish in ice, the purpose being to keep them from becoming too dry as frozen fish tend to.

In recent years I have been filleting all the fish I clean, bass or otherwise. This eliminates the pesky bones that make eating fish as much of a chore as a pleasure. All you need is a sharp fillet knife and a board or some other flat surface to work on. I learned this method years ago from a Canadian walleye fishing guide, and I now use it on all fish. Place the bass one side down on the board, hold its head with one hand, and do the filleting with the other. Make a cut right behind the gill covers all the way to the backbone, and then turn the knife sideways with the edge toward the tail. Now cut carefully along the backbone toward the tail. This frees one fillet. Stop just before you reach the tail, leaving a piece of skin which attaches the fillet to the fish. Flip the fillet over and now work back toward the head between the skin and the meat. This removes one fillet which is ready for the pan — or the freezer. Turn the bass over and repeat this procedure on the other side.

Some anglers prefer to cook the whole fish, and if they do, they will need to first scale the fish. To do so they need pliers or special fish-cleaning grippers to hold the fish by the tail, a scaler, and a good knife. The fillet knife is fine, but not really necessary. It just needs to be sharp. To scale place the fish on the flat surface, grip it by the tail with pliers or a gripper, and with the scaler work against the scales all the way to the gill covers. Do this on both sides. Now make a cut along the belly from the gill covers to the anus opening, and remove the viscera. Also chop off the head, and using the point of the knife remove the blood from each side of the backbone. The fish is now ready to go into the pan.

There's a lot of satisfaction from turning a fine bass or a catch of bass into delicious food ready for the table. That's part of what fishing is all about.

Chapter XI
Farm Ponds

"We need a story on the three top bass waters in the state," said the editor. "Big bass."

The discussion rolled on, and my mind began to spin. Lake Gaston on the North Carolina-Virginia border has a reputation for big largemouth bass. It once held the record in both states.

Just upstream on the same river is 50,000-acre Buggs Island, the largest lake in Virginia. It has been making fishing headlines — yielding sizable bass. Briery Creek, a Virginia Department of Game and Inland Fisheries lake in Prince Edward County is a new lake, but getting a lot of attention from bass anglers. Much smaller, but I couldn't ignore it.

Each of the lakes would make incredible story material, but I was only speculating that these were among the best bass-fishing waters in the state.

Major bass waters in any state seem to rotate big-bass honors from season to season. Even pollution-plagued and now all but dead Back Bay rode the crest one memorable year.

Surely, Lakes Gaston or Buggs Island would claim either first or second place at the present. But to my surprise, the records of the Department of Game and Inland Fisheries pointed in a totally unexpected direction. Now all-but-dead Back Bay was easily number one that distant year — but the second place slot belonged to the farm ponds — collectively. Those tiny impoundments scattered about the state had a solid lock on the number two spot.

"A lot of farm ponds are underfished," said fisheries biologist Jack Hoffman. "Most are privately owned, and

Young anglers often catch good bass from farm ponds.

fishing is often limited to the owner and his family or friends. Some of those bass live to an old age."

The more experienced anglers, those who fish primarily from bass boats equipped with the latest in electronic fishing aids, rarely fish farm ponds. In fact, they can't launch their boats on most of them.

Older bass become more selective in those little waters, feed only when they are in the mood, and seldom work for their dinner bells. Farm ponds usually become overpopulated with stunted bluegills which provide for easy forage for big, growing bass.

There's no better place than a farm pond for a budding bass angler to kick off his angling career. The chances are good he will catch his first bass ever on that very first trip.

Fishing a farm pond is rarely complicated. You don't need a bass boat with its sophisticated equipment, though it might be helpful. But on most farm ponds, launching such a craft would be a major logistic problem. These little fishing trips to nearby ponds are not necessarily all-day outings; it's fishing to be squeezed into a tight schedule — after school or work, before school or work, or even during the work day. I've run into anglers fishing farm ponds on their lunch hours — chomping on a sandwich, but casting as they did so. A cane pole, light monofilament line, hook, and a live minnow and you are in business. You might want to use a bobber to keep the minnow above the tops of bottom vegetation and a sinker to keep it from swimming to the top — but nothing more. Millions of largemouth bass have been caught on such humble tackle, but you will probably prefer to go with your spinning tackle as described in Chapter II.

Most farm-pond anglers fish from the shore. That goes with the convenience. No bother with cartopping or trailering a boat, inflating a raft, or unfolding a portable rig. Just walk to the pond, make yourself comfortable, and cast out a line.

Bank anglers often catch nice bass, some even trophy-size. It is not, however, the best way to fish a pond. For one thing, the bank fisherman presents a high profile, spooking many bass. As he walks to the edge of a pond, he may see swirls as alarmed fish move to deeper water.

Frogs are common to farm ponds and bass feed on them.

There are several things the bank fisherman can do to minimize the effects of his profile on the fishing. Treading softly helps. This has nothing to do with the angler's profile, but those heavy footsteps apparently create vibrations which the bass can detect, particularly those close to the shore. Combined with that sudden profile out there on the bank, they can send bass scurrying. One way to reduce the adverse effects of the profile is to make sure the sun doesn't cast your shadow on the water. Walk into the sun if possible, or with it to your side. Never approach a pond with the sun to your back.

My favorite approach to fishing farm ponds is to wade near the shore, casting ahead and out to the deeper water. I prefer to wear chest waders, but you can wade wet if the water isn't too cold and you don't object to wading over muddy bottoms. The bottoms of most farm ponds are pretty mushy. The most important advantage of wading is the reduction of your profile. Knee-deep in water, the angler is much less conspicuous than when he's standing on the bank. Wading also allows the angler to work lures parallel to the shoreline, exposing them to fish feeding in the shallows. Aside from the angling advantages that wading offers, there is less risk of picking up chiggers and ticks. Both are common around farm ponds, particularly those in cattle country.

The shoreline water of most farm ponds is shallow enough to wade, but if it is not, you can use a float tube. You can climb into it and get through water too deep to wade. Even in shallow water it's a good safety precaution. The bottoms of most farm ponds tend to drop off rather rapidly. They are built that way. A reason later.

Other options include light jon boats, two-man bass boats — or one-man ones, folding boats, canoes, and rafts. You may want to mount a small electric motor on a boat or canoe, but most farm ponds are so small that a motor is really unnecessary — mostly an unnecessary bother.

Anglers who take the time to study a farm pond during its construction will better understand how to fish the pond. The basins of most are bulldozed clean, and the earth is used to build the dam. A completed farm pond has little or no structure in it. Rarely are there boulders, fallen trees, standing timber, or other structure to provide cover for the fish.

As indicated earlier, shallow water is also limited — and for a reason. Shallows allow bluegills and other panfish to escape the predatory bass. As a result the panfish become overpopulated and stunted. Pond owners rely upon bass to keep other sunfish populations in check. The Soil Conservation Service, which designs and provides advice on farm-pond construction, generally recommends very limited shallow area.

Ponds change with time, however, as debris collects in the water, fallen trees add cover and logs float in from the

A good catch of bass from a farm pond. The angler used both casting and spinning tackle.

hinterland during floods. The shore begins to fill in a bit to provide more extensive shallows. But this general knowledge of pond construction can prove helpful to the angler fishing a strange pond. He knows generally what to expect. A chat with the landowner might also help — providing, of course, that he was the owner when the pond was built.

Otherwise, probe the bottom with plastic worms or deep-running lures to explore the fish-catching possibilities. A depth finder can be of help here. You can even mount it on a jon boat and check out the various depths. It will probably also show locations of structure — if such exist.

Generally, regardless of its size or contour, three good fishing areas exist in a pond. One is near the mouths of feeder streams — no matter how tiny the stream might be. Some ponds may appear to have no feeder streams, but don't be misled. Often there is only one, the impounded one. Even it may dry up during prolonged spells of dry weather. This could be a mere trickle of water, but don't overlook it. These feeder streams, regardless of their size, wash all kinds of food into the pond. This is particularly true during floods. Those tiny tricklets can becoming raging waters. Panfish congregate where they enter the pond and feast on the sudden influx of food. The bass then move in to feed on the exposed panfish.

Another good spot is near the drain pipe, usually visible near the dam. Water being sucked into the pipe also collects food, and again you have the food-bluegill-bass combination. During periods of dry weather the level of many ponds may sink below drainage level and water will discontinue flowing through the drain. Food won't be drawn to it, but bass are often found loafing or feeding near the pipe, sometimes deep. Never overlook this possibility regardless of the weather.

A third hot spot in farm ponds, but certainly not the least productive one, is the dam itself. Most are earth dams, built from earth scooped out of the pond basin. The base of the dam is usually wide — 20 to 30 feet — depending on how high the dam is, and it gradually slopes down from top to bottom. A lure worked slowly down the slope is almost a sure bet, one that will get attention.

It takes time to learn a pond and fish it effectively. Most ponds are 10 to 20 feet deep with the deepest water in the middle and near the dam. Lunker bass usually hold in these areas, particularly during hot weather. Work plastic worms or hop lures along the bottom in this part of a pond. Although few new ponds have vegetation, the earliest growth is near the shore. Cattails are the most common new vegetation. Spinnerbaits or surface lures worked along the edges of such vegetation usually produce action. Most bass caught near the vegetation tend to be small, but at times larger bass feed in the vegetation — particularly early and late in the day when they cruise the pond on feeding forays.

Pond owners may build small docks for their boats, and this type of structure often provides shelter for largemouth bass. If you plan to fish around a boat secured to a dock or the dock itself, first stand back to cast and work a lure around and under it.

In some parts of the country, where rainfall is adequate, the water level is maintained by runoff. "Catch basins" they are called. Others, however, are fed by springs that were inundated when the ponds were formed.

No experienced bass angler needs to be told the cooler water near these springs can be one of the best fishing holes in the pond. The pond owner may be willing to point them out to you. Otherwise, you'll have to search for them. If the water is clear enough, the presence of lush aquatic vegetation may reveal their locations. Farm pond water, unfortunately, is seldom that clear.

One beauty of farm ponds is that they are small enough that you can cover most of the water in a few hours of fishing. Be sure to make mental notes to remember where the best action is. Commit the mental notes to paper as soon as possible and file them for future use.

The millions of farm ponds across America are easy to

fish and fairly easy to establish a pattern on, or otherwise come up with a fishing plan that will produce bass. In many states they move ahead of larger, more popular waters in producing trophy-size bass.

We've spent a lot of time talking about farm ponds and how to fish them, but how do you find them, and once you find them how do you get permission to fish them? After all, most are on private land.

If you live in a rural area or even a small town, locating farm ponds is rarely a problem. In fact, you probably already know the location of several. Now, it's just a matter of getting permission to fish one of them. Anglers living in large cities do have a problem. For one thing they may have to drive for several miles beyond the city limits to even get into farming country.

One good approach is to contact the Soil Conservation Agent in the county you are interested in and solicit his help. He probably has a map showing the locations of all ponds in the county. For many of those ponds he may have designed and supervised the construction of the dams. He's also on speaking terms with the owners, and may know who will allow fishing and who will not. Generally, however, don't expect him to intercede for you. Thank him for the information and ask for or buy a map if one is available.

If the county conservation agent doesn't have maps check with the highway or transportation department, usually at the state level. Topographical maps available from the U. S. Geological Survey may show a few farm ponds, but certainly not all of them. Probably your best bet is to get a map of the county and plot in the ponds. The conservation agent may be willing to help you with this.

Over the long term you don't want to abuse the privilege if you can get permission of fish a particular pond. A much better approach is to locate several of them and rotate among them, fishing any one only two or three times a season. Some will offer better fishing than others, but even so don't concentrate on one or two of the best ones.

Common courtesy will keep those ponds open for your bass fishing pleasure. You may want to keep a few bass, but limit the number you kill for the table. Ask the owner if he has any concerns about keeping bass. Some like for visiting anglers to keep all of the bluegills they catch, but release all of the bass. Discuss this with the pond owner.

Did the owner give you permission, and you only? Or does he object if you bring a friend? Regardless, don't take a crowd of friends with you.

Ask the owner if he would like some fish for the table. If he does, don't hand him a stringer of bass or bluegills to clean. Take them home, clean them and then deliver them to the pond owner.

And keep in mind that farm ponds are not public water, nor are they stocked with public funds. At one time various federal and state agencies did provide fingerlings for new ponds, but I don't believe this is the practice anymore — at any level of government. Farm ponds are a private effort from buying the land and building the pond to stocking it with fingerling fish — and fertilizing it. The better farm ponds are fertilized periodically if the fish are to develop appreciable size.

Even so farm ponds can provide many hours of good bass fishing — even by those who do not own them.

A folding boat is ideal for fishing farm ponds.

Chapter XII
Canals and Ditches

Following a few days on the North Carolina beaches, I had convinced my family we should move inland and see some different kind of country before our vacation ended. That was years ago, but as always, I had stored my fishing tackle in the back of the station wagon. Always prepared if a fishing opportunity presented itself. I had even found a few freshwater ponds back of the sand dunes in Nags Head and caught a couple of small bass. I fished them from the banks along with several other hopeful anglers.

Driving inland from the Outer Banks of North Carolina you crossed Albemarle Sound, by a ferry then, but now by bridge. As you do so you enter a vast wilderness area of marshes, scrub timber, swamps, and endless canals and ditches. Most are along the highways. They were formed when the roads were constructed in the wilderness wetlands. It's wild, picturesque country—and forbidding. Get lost in that back country and you are in trouble. In recent years it has become possibly the most productive bear hunting country in eastern America.

But it was those ditches along the highway that caught my angler's eye. Mile after mile of dark, mysterious water. It didn't seem to flow, but there is always some current in those ditches—barely perceptible. This was bass fishing country and I just knew those waters held largemouth bass.

My wife and two daughters didn't thrill to that drive the way I did, and perhaps couldn't understand my fascination with it.

Late that afternoon we checked into a picturesque lodge that obviously catered to anglers and hunters—mostly

Canals and ditches are often fished from the banks.

waterfowl hunters. Nearby was some of the best duck and goose hunting in America. The owner of the lodge, however, was a bass angler, and it didn't take me long to begin pumping him.

"Good white perch fishing in the ditches now," he offered.

Sure, I like to fish for white perch, but those miles of murky water had me thinking bass. They would be fairly easy to fish. The highway shoulders were wide and the traffic was light. I could hardly wait to break out my fly rod and toss some bugs on its dark waters.

"I'm about the only bass fisherman around here," said our host. "We have another lodge further inland and I drive back and forth a lot. Always have my fly rod along," he added, pointing to the back of his big station wagon.

We talked awhile until duty eventually called him elsewhere. But not until he had confirmed my belief that some good bass finned those stained waters. "Mostly cypress stain," he said.

"One of my favorite places is at either end of a road culvert," he told me. "But you have to stand way back so the bass don't spook."

There was just enough time to get in an hour of fishing before dinner, and I excused myself and headed out.

It didn't take me long to locate a productive-looking culvert. It was actually a corrugated metal pipe about 18 inches in diameter. There was probably at least a foot of water in the pipe, plenty of depth for bass to swim through moving from one ditch to the other across the highway. I got close enough to determine this—hopefully without disturbing the bass.

Standing well back, but still on the broad shoulder of the road, I worked out some fly line and dropped a big popping bug as quietly as I could about a foot out from the mouth of the culvert. Nothing. Ever so gently I worked the bug creating a little ripple on the surface of the water. That did it! The water suddenly boiled and I felt the strength and weight of a good fish on my willowy rod. The outcome was in doubt for awhile, but eventually I worked the fish to the bank of the ditch—a nice two-pounder.

A Small bass taken from a Louisiana canal.

At daybreak the next morning I was back on those ditches along both sides of the highway. I broke away to fish as frequently as I could during our brief stay at the lodge. The culverts proved to be the high percentage waters. I could almost assure myself of action there, but the fish hit all along the highway.

Yes, I was fishing with a fly rod, but I was well along in my bass fishing career then. I could have done just as well with a long cane pole that allowed me to stand back from the water and fish

The largemouth is the usual bass found in canals and ditches.

lively minnows in those waters. You don't have to speculate on how productive that method would have been. Fantastic. I could also have tied a small surface lure on a light spinning outfit and placed myself even further back from the water—and probably been more productive than I was with the fly rod.

Canals and ditches. Man-made waters, and you find them all over America. They serve all kinds of purposes—carrying water from one body to another, drainage, irrigation, long-neglected canals that in yesteryears funneled water to water-powered mills, or served river transportation permitting boats to by-pass shoals and other unnavigable water, and so on. About the only limit on such waters is man's imagination or engineering ingenuity. Some are highly controversial, those that drain wetlands, for example.

Despite this, many are good bass fishing water. Most are overlooked. Seldom fished. They can be a gold mine for the enterprising bass angler. Many are on public property such as those along major highways. Getting permission to fish even those on private property is seldom difficult. It may never have occurred to the owner that the water you want to test was worthy of fishing attention.

The largemouth bass particularly is a highly adaptable critter. Give it reasonably clean water with moderate depths, some forage fish, and it will survive and often prosper. Canals and ditches of various kinds furnish this need.

Even seasonal water can be productive if bass have access to permanent waters. It's surprising how bass will move temporarily into new waters. True, they are sometimes trapped there, but rarely.

I happened to stumble upon an angler who was familiar with those North Carolina ditches, but more often the only way to find out whether they hold bass is to fish them. Several times if at first you don't succeed. The bass is a moody fish that doesn't always feed—even when you drop a juicy minnow before its snout.

If you locate some good canals or ditches it may be prudent to keep your secret to yourself and a few close friends. Many of these waters are small and cannot stand a lot of fishing pressure.

Also keep your eyes peeled for "no fishing" signs. Sometimes private owners want to limit the fishing to themselves and their friends. Even then you might be able to get permission to fish by approaching the owner. Public property managers may also post their waters for safety reasons. They don't want to get hit with a lawsuit by someone who is injured on their property. This may be purely a precautionary measure, and the manager could care less if you fish. That posted sign becomes his defense if presented with a summons to court. You have to play these by ear and figure out for yourself what the actual intent is. At the worst you are likely fishing at your own risk.

That's the nature of canals and ditches that hold bass, and there are countless such waters that offer good bass fishing.

One of the beauties of fishing canals and ditches is the limited amount of equipment you need. Generally, it's bank fishing pure and simple. You don't need a boat, nor even boots or waders. In fact, a boat could be a hindrance, and waders could get you in trouble where there is deep water. Some of those highway ditches are 10 feet or more in depth in places.

Get together a limited selection of fishing tackle and you are ready to fish. While you don't need boots or waders, shoes that don't leak can sometimes be a comfort. The footing can be muddy or wet or the morning dew heavy on the grass.

I suppose I am thinking mostly in terms of highway ditches, generally the most accessible ones, and there bank fishing is a good way to go. There are canals and ditches, however, that run deep into near-wilderness areas. In fact, some of those ditches in the North Carolina coastal country lead deep into the wilderness swamps. They are probably best fished by a small boat. A light jon boat would be ideal, but a canoe could also be used.

When fishing from the broad shoulder of a busy highway, safety demands that you keep in mind the traffic flowing by behind you. You certainly don't want to get excited and step backwards into the path of a moving vehicle.

If fishing with a fly rod, and to a lesser extent with a casting or spinning rod, you have to watch your back cast. Florida is well known for its highway ditches that attract anglers. I recall years ago reading the story of a fly fisherman working a highway ditch. He apparently forgot about his back cast and unfortunately snagged a passing automobile. How, I don't recall. Possibly he wrapped his leader around a radio antenna. In any event he was suddenly flipped over backwards and was saved from serious injury only because his leader broke. The automobile was unscathed, but the story didn't tell how the angler and his tackle fared. Hopefully, only his dignity was damaged.

It behooves the angler to learn as much as he can about

the canal or ditch he plans to fish—as in fishing all waters. I'm not talking about ownership here. We've already covered that. But about the depth of the water, vegetation, underwater structure such as submerged trees, docks and other such matter, the location of any springs that might feed into the water or actually spring up at its bottom. Such knowledge can lead you to better fishing. It's also well to learn where the canal or ditch originates and where it ends—even though the beginning or end might be miles away. What kinds of fish are in that water it feeds or drains. And for that matter what kind of fish are found in the canal or ditch—other than bass.

You should also try to determine what kind of forage fish the water holds. And what other food for the bass. Many of these canals or ditches, particularly those in low country, are loaded with frogs of all ages from tadpoles on up. The bass are obviously alert for such food, particularly a young frog leaping from one bank and swimming desperately for the far one. Insect life can be an important food source in these waters so often near grassy areas or beneath overhanging vegetation.

Learning the depth of the water and being able to distinguish between the deeper water and the shallows can also boost your angling opportunities. This is true in all waters, but on larger ones you often have maps or depth finders to help you. These bass are not different than those in the big reservoirs for the most part. They move into the shallows to feed, but use the deep water for protection and as an escape area.

Generally, you will find canal and ditch bass in the shallows early and late in the day and at night, and in the deeper water at midday, but not always. Such waters are often well shaded and the fish may feed in the shallows throughout the day. They are not bothered as much by the sun as they would be in more open waters.

Any docks along the canal? You often come across them. Good cover for bass, and a good spot from which to fish. If a cottage or house is nearby ask before you use it.

Grassy areas, particularly in the South, are often infested with chiggers and ticks, so go prepared. Tuck the bottoms of your trousers into your socks and spray well with insect repellent. And don't relax in those clothes once you are back home. Take them off immediately and hang them out for a few days. Any pests clinging to them will soon drop off. Once your clothes are removed inspect your body thoroughly for ticks. You won't be able to see chiggers for awhile, but if they are there they will soon make their presence known.

One of the advantages of fishing canals and ditches is the accessibility of the water. In most instances you can stand on one side and cast to the far bank with ease—even with a fly rod. This is rare when you fish even farm ponds from the banks. Every inch of that canal or ditch is easily fished. In few other instances is that the case when fishing from the bank.

A disadvantage of fishing canals and ditches from the bank is snagging lures—either on underwater obstacles or overhanging tree branches. In both cases it means a lost lure unless you can pull it free. Sometimes you can, but no always. If the water isn't too deep you can wade in and free your lure, but do so carefully. The muck in some of those canals and ditches seems almost bottomless. Test it before you plant a foot firmly for the next step.

There may be more interesting waters to fish, but I doubt it. There's something challenging and mysterious about those dank, dark waters that you find in few other places.

Canals and ditches along highways are never hard to find. Drive through the South, for example, particularly in the flat country near the coast and you will see miles and miles of them—much more water than you will live long enough to fish.

Many years ago I used to drive from my home in central Virginia to the resort city of Virginia Beach. As we left the rolling hill country and entered the flat coastal plains the ditches along the highway began to appear. They fascinated me in those distant days, and they still do today.

In the years since, I have had the opportunity to fish many of these canals and ditches and generally they fulfill my expectations.

Once an angler has viewed the generally still waters of a dark, mysterious canal or ditch, he won't be happy until he has had the opportunity to fish one. And the best part is that he can do so at a minimum of cost.

If a boat is needed to fish a canal or ditch a jon boat is just about ideal.

Chapter XIII
Millponds and Small Lakes

Millponds. Idyllic waters. Once the very epitome of bass fishing waters. So much so that early writers took the liberty of combining mill and pond into one word.

Millponds are lingering symbols of an earlier era when farmers took their grain to the mills and had it ground into flour, meal, and other products for the farm or home. They were seldom large bodies of water. A 10-acre millpond was a big one, but did they offer some prime bass fishing! I caught my first largemouth in the headwaters of a millpond more years ago than I like to recall, but those memories are sweet. This old millpond was formed back in the Great Depression when an enterprising miller built a dam downstream on the little creek that flowed through the family farm. He wasn't a fisherman himself and when a group of city anglers offered to buy the fishing rights to the pond he jumped at the opportunity. That put it off limits to the kids in the neighborhood, but fortunately the dam pushed the headwaters above the property of the miller and onto the land of one of our neighbors. That gave us kids access to at least part of the pond, and we caught untold numbers of bass from its waters.

The bass released in the pond prospered, and young fish often worked their way up the creek to the stretch that ran through our property. They were hard to catch there in the shallow pools, but we enjoyed the challenge — and the fish.

The dam of that old pond eventually broke and the millpond disappeared for awhile, but eventually an heir of the miller acquired the property, rebuilt the dam and put the mill back into operation. That time the fishing worked

Old millponds are often rich in largemouth bass.

out better for the local anglers as the heir retained the fishing rights and allowed his customers to fish. Unfortunately the dam broke again during a hurricane and accompanying flood. The pond no longer exists, but I learned a lot about fishing in that old millpond, and even built a crude wooden boat and picked up the basics of bass fishing from a boat.

Despite the off-and-on history of that millpond, some old ones still exist around the nation, particularly in the bass country of the South. They are rich bodies of water noted for big bass. Many are open to the public — often sometimes for a fee. They are worth checking out.

Millponds are often fished from the shore, but modern light boats such as jon boats can be launched on most of them. If there is no launching area they can be scooted down a grassy bank.

Millponds were particularly popular among anglers of

yesterday — back in the days before the proliferation of big reservoirs. Often they offered the only largemouth bass fishing available in some communities.

The expert anglers usually fished the millponds in teams, one angler paddling the boat, working in and out of coves, along weedy shorelines, and putting the angler in the bow of the boat next to the best cover he could find. The angler worked the shoreline with either casting or fly tackle, and periodically the two swapped positions, the angler moving to the stern to paddle for awhile while the other took his go at the fishing. It was a highly productive and enjoyable way to fish for bass.

All anglers, of course, did not use artificial lures. Many simply anchored their boat in water known to hold bass and stood guard over a battery of long cane poles. Both live minnows and worms took bass in those days. Locating the best bass waters was mostly by trial and error. Good holes located in this manner were often well-kept secrets.

Some of these ancient millponds may be convenient to your own home. Check out the possibility. Even if they are posted with "no fishing" signs, they may be open for a modest fee. If so the fishing could be well worth it.

Many are accessible from the banks, but for better access to the pond either rent a boat or launch your own boat or raft. Often the fishing fee will include the use of a boat. If so take advantage of it. Millponds are best fished from a boat, as bank access usually restricts you to a small section of the water — possibly the least productive.

Fishing a millpond calls for no particular techniques. Those that will catch bass just about anywhere will do so in these little impoundments. These ponds are old, many of them are, well past the century mark, and they have taken on many of the characteristics of natural bodies of water. Aquatic vegetation in the form of weed beds and lily pads are common, and they demand the attention of the bass angler. Work them hard and thoroughly, particularly early and late in the day when the fish are feeding. If you locate a particularly good spot, mark it by triangulation, using shoreline points as markers.

117

Jerry Almy with a nice largemouth taken from a tiny pond on a Virginia military reservation.

The headwaters of a millpond is always worth checking out. Fresh water pours in here, filled with oxygen and food. It's a good place to spend some time. There may be smaller streams, spring branches for example, that enter the pond. They too attract bass roaming for food.

In the newer millponds there may still be standing timber — long since dead. Such cover attracts all kinds of insects which attract small fish which in turn attract bass.

In some parts of the country strip mining and quarry operations create small lakes. Once abandoned, they fill with water from springs, run-off, or diverted streams. They are often overlooked possibilities for bass fishing. The strip mining pits of Southeastern Kansas are noted for their fine fishing. Some of these pits were initially poor for fishing because of infertile soil, poor water quality and a paucity of shallow water for feeding and spawning, but good management has improved many of them. It's a point to keep in mind, however. All strip mining pits and quarries are not good for fishing. The only way to find out is to fish them.

Quarries and pits vary greatly as to depth. Some are shallow, but others are very deep. Some have steep banks while others slope gently.

While I was a student at the University of Virginia, one

Anglers fish an old millpond.

of my classmates, an incurable fishermen, tired of studying one afternoon, picked up his fishing tackle, and hiked across a field near his living quarters to try his luck in a long-abandoned quarry. A couple of casts and he tied into one of the largest bass he'd ever caught. Naturally, that quarry immediately got a lot of attention, but it didn't prove highly productive. That big old bass had probably been ruling the dark, deep waters of that abandoned rock quarry for a number of seasons, but he didn't enjoy a lot of company. Even so this episode points out the wisdom of checking out overlooked waters occasionally instead of joining the crowd at the nearby hard-fished reservoir.

Mining acids might prove too strong for fish to survive in some mining pits, but state fisheries agencies can often handle this to convert unproductive waters into highly productive ones. Rock quarries are less likely to be acidic than strip mining pits.

Fishing quarries and pits often means fishing deeper than you do in millponds. Keep this in mind as you explore new waters.

Anglers traveling Interstate 81 through western Pennsylvania will see a goodly number of abandoned mining pits brimming full with sparkling water. I've thrilled to these prospective waters many times over the years, but have not yet found the time to check them out. I have noticed activity on some — docks, and launching ramps. Obviously there is some fishing there. Others appear to get little attention. I assume the waters in those are too acidic for fish. But that's just a guess. It does show, however, how new waters catch an angler's eye. I dare say most people traveling that busy highway never give a thought to those waters. In my case it demonstrates how a mature bass angler is always alert for new fishing possibilities.

It is interesting to note that the fishing possibilities these mining and quarries offer are not overlooked by state fisheries people. Biologists in Kansas, for example, increase the shallow water areas in some pits by building dams to raise and spread the water.

While we are on the subject of fisheries management, it is interesting to note that most state agencies build lakes just to be managed for fishing — and rarely are these lakes large ones. Size is relative, of course, but in Virginia the Department of Game and Inland Fisheries over the years has built several dozen lakes just for fishing. They range in size from a small 19-acre one to the most recently built one which is over 800 acres. This is so in many states. Check with your own fisheries agency. Compare these fishing waters to giant reservoirs in the 10,000 to 50,000-

acre category. Giant bodies of water are not needed to offer good fishing, and the smaller ones are easier to manage.

Several years back I wrote a guide on Virginia's fishing waters. Chapters were devoted to large streams, small streams, large lakes, small ones and so on. It was a convenient way to organize the vast array of fishing waters in the state, but I had trouble arriving at a breaking point between large lakes and small ones. I eventually put all lakes and ponds under 500 acres in the small category. Arbitrary of course, but it proved workable. There were almost 200 small lakes and ponds, however, and the impact they have on fishing in Virginia is immeasurable.

Both farm ponds and lakes built by the state fisheries agencies are actually small impoundments, and I'm always fascinated by the water immediately below the dams, tailwaters of the dam if you prefer. This can be highly productive. Sometimes it is open to the public for fishing, but not always. Check this before you test it.

Several things make this water productive. For one thing it holds bass from both downstream and upstream above the dam. The fish from downstream, moving upstream, are blocked from further travel by the dam. They apparently find the water acceptable and take up residence there—at least temporarily. Those from the lake move over the overflow area during periods of floods and high water. They too find the tailwaters attractive. Generally there is an abundance of forage fish, and the waters pouring over the dam create a good supply of oxygen.

There is almost always a good tailwaters pool below the dam. Just how deep and large it is depends mostly upon the amount of water coming over the dam and churning out the stream bed. It also fluctuates. A heavy flood, for example, might churn out a good pool which will gradually fill in during periods of dry weather or drouths.

Over the years I've found the tailwaters of lakes and ponds so attractive I often fish there before moving on to the impounded water above. The fish are of necessity concentrated in the usually small pools, and they are not that difficult to locate.

Largemouth bass taken from a small Minnesota lake.

There's an ancient millpond in Virginia's Cumberland County that I used to fish fairly frequently. One early morning as I was driving to the launching area, I happened to glance at the little stream just below the lake, its tailwaters. The country road continued by crossing the stream just below the dam and beneath that bridge was a pool I couldn't resist. I parked on the shoulder of the road, got out my casting rod and eased down the bank to the edge of the pool. My first cast hit a bridge abutment and the lure dropped quietly on the water. I believe my lure was the popular Jitterbug. In any event, I let it rest on the surface a minute and the wiggled it just slightly. The pool literally exploded as the fish hit. Surprised, I was late striking, but the fish set the hooks itself and I spent a good five minutes fighting and landing one of the largest largemouth bass of my career. Never overlook those tailwaters.

If you happen to locate a good private pond or lake nearby and get permission to fish it, you can help some with its management. This will insure good fishing for years. One good way is to periodically take a bag of fertilizer or lime and dump it into the feeder stream just upstream from the lake. A bass angler can do much toward having good water to fish by lending a helping hand to a pond or lake owner trying to manage his water for better fishing. In this modern day of heavy demands on most of our resources, the better fishing waters are managed.

There are all kinds of small lakes and pond across America. Sometimes fishing clubs build them for their members, land developers build them to make their projects more attractive to prospective buyers, and there are community lakes for swimming and other water sports. You will find them in state parks, and highway construction has created lakes, some of them sizeable. Just drive a major interstate highway across the Midwest and take note of the lakes where major highways cross the interstate. Lakes have been created where earth was removed to provide material for the huge fillings at interchanges. Most anglers are aware of these fine lakes. Most are reasonably shallow and generallly accessible. Some are on private land where the owners vary in their attitudes toward fishing. Some, however, are on public land. Check these possibilities out also.

Water supply reservoirs for the major cities are usually large bodies of water, many of which are open for fishing. Most fall in the large lake or reservoir category which we will discuss later, but there are thousands of small ones which differ little from the small lakes we have already discussed. For public safety the authorities usually retain some control over the fishing, but not to the extent that it is prohibited.

If you are a golfer you are aware of the many small ponds or lakes that dot most courses. Did it ever occur to you that these might hold bass?

It has always puzzled me that newcomers to bass fishing buy their equipment and head first to some big reservoir that every angler in the area knows about. Sort of following the crowd. But in traveling to and from those big bodies of water, they cross or pass numerous small waters that get little or no attention from anglers. These are waters that are much easier to fish and do not require a heavy investment in a boat and equipment that the big waters usually do.

Check out some of those little lakes and ponds, and you may find the fishing so good that you'll not even consider making the trip to the bigger, but more crowded, reservoir or lake, particularly during the hot summer months when sun reflected off of that broad surface can be unmerciful.

Chapter XIV
Small Streams

I learned to fish in a small stream, a creek we called it, but small streams take many names creeks, cricks, runs, and even rivers. I've seen some river headwaters that were smaller than the creek where I spent so many delightful boyhood days. Little waters you can jump across. The stream I have in mind is generally too small to fish from a boat or canoe, one best fished by wading. There are millions of them that ribbon just about every part of America. Some, of course, are trout streams, but there are also an equal number or possibly even more that are too warm for trout. Many of these hold

Largemouth bass work into small streams from farm ponds in their drainage system.
(Storm Manufacturing Company.)

bass, either largemouth, smallmouth, or spotted bass.

One of the joys of fishing small streams is the ease with which you can approach the fishing. Rod, reel, and a small kit of lures and you're ready. No complications. Wade wet if you like or pull on hip boots or waders. The typical small stream is a tributary of a larger one. In fact it may be a tributary of a tributary. Or even three or four times removed from the main stream which forms a river basin. This means there is usually a fair amount of fast water. No I don't mean class III rapids that thrill white-water canoeists, but instead mild rapids or even riffles. They are usually shallow and sometimes referred to as shoals. Over a given stretch of stream, the fast water in the way of rapids and riffles will alternate with quiet pools. Depending upon the kind of bass you are fishing for, each kind of water has its attractions.

Part of the success of fishing small streams is being able to read the current. Stream bass tend to look to the current for food. It's usually well laden with a rich variety in the way of insects, tiny or struggling frogs, dying minnows or bait fish, and various other forms of life the bass feed on. Even small animals. Young birds often tumble from a nest above the stream and offer a choice meal for a hungry bass.

Study those rapids and riffles and note where the main current pours into the pool below. Floating debris, leaves, and other matter will follow the current.

For much of the day the bass will be concentrated in those sparkling pools, usually the deeper ones. This eliminates a lot of water, and you can concentrate on the most productive. But feeding time, usually early and late in the day, sees the bass moving out of the deeper water into the shallows and even into the shoals to feed. That indicates a change in tactics.

Good cover, or structure as bass anglers tend to call it, is more obvious in a small stream. Look for submerged logs, piles of debris near the banks, weed beds, boulders, fallen trees, and other such cover. Bass often rest in the quiet water below such cover because it breaks the current and they can rest more easily.

Bends in the stream are also worthy of attention, particularly the bank on the outside of the turn. The current slams into the bank here and often carves out a deep hole plus holes beneath the bank. Undercut banks they are called, and every stream fisherman recognizes their value.

Learn to understand the current and the various kinds

Hip boots will get an angler into most of the water in a small stream.
(Ginny Gooch photo.)

of cover in a stream, and you are well along toward becoming a good stream fisherman.

It's well to keep in mind that small streams can rise quickly with a heavy rainfall. They also become muddy and all but impossible to fish. Watch the weather and plan your trips accordingly. While small streams can get muddy very quickly, they also clear up very quickly. Give a flooding small stream two or three days and the fishing can return to normal.

The great majority of small streams in America flow through private land. Depending upon the applicable state laws, the stream may be considered either private property or property of the state and thus open to the public. The latter situation is becoming more prevalent, but be sure of its status before you fish a stream. In any event, it's often necessary to cross private property to reach a stream, and this may require the consent of the landowner. If in doubt always ask. Showing this courtesy to a landowner always leaves a better taste in his mouth.

Want to determine what kind of bass you are likely to find in a small stream? Study both its headwaters and the country downstream from it.

Let's look downstream first. That will give you a better clue as to the native bass in the stream. Get a good map of the area, particularly of the stream basin, and trace the stream to its confluence with a larger stream. Ideally you should trace the stream, and those it enters, to the main stream in the river basin. Bass tend to work upstream, particularly smallmouth bass. If that main or mother stream holds a good smallmouth bass population, you are almost sure to catch some smallmouths in its tributaries — way upstream. One of my favorite small streams is the tributary of a tributary of a tributary which flows into Virginia's James River, one of the best smallmouth bass streams in America. I almost always catch smallmouths when I fish that little stream. If that major river is a good largemouth stream, expect to catch largemouths in its tributaries, but there is a better clue to the likely presence of largemouth bass in a small stream. We'll get to that shortly.

128

The Kentucky or spotted bass is also a good stream fish. In fact I first met this fine bass in a small stream in southern Kansas, a spring-fed stream that flowed through private property. I had to get the permission of a farmer to fish the stream, but had no problem. If there are spotted bass downstream there are almost sure to be some in the smaller waters upstream. That Kansas stream I fished was small enough to leap across.

Having studied the downstream water, now turn your attention upstream. It is here that you will get a better indication of what the largemouth bass fishing is like. Are there farm ponds or other small impoundments in the drainage? If so they are most likely stocked with largemouth bass and these fish have a habit of escaping their impounded waters and working downstream. This most often occurs during floods that cause the impoundments to overflow. The refugee bass often settle in more or less once they reach a good pool in some small stream. The largemouth bass prefers the quieter water whereas the smallmouth is addicted to faster water. Usually you will find both kinds of water in a small stream and if there are smallmouths in a larger river downstream and impounded waters in the watershed, you are almost sure to find both largemouth and smallmouth bass in the small stream you plan to fish.

While the two bass prefer different kinds of water and cover you may often find them in the same pool. It's not unusual to catch a largemouth on one cast and a smallmouth on the next. That's one of the joys of fishing a small stream.

Locating these small streams is seldom a problem. In fact, you are probably already aware of several of them, streams you've crossed dozens of times as you drive through the country. You probably have never given them a second thought, feeling they are too small to fish.

A more organized approach, however, can begin with an official state highway map. It won't show all of the small streams in the state, but many of them will appear as thin blue lines. All of the major rivers will be there, however, and

129

Author prefers chest waders even in small steams as they will allow him to reach water hip boots would not.   (Ginny Gooch photo.)

Author tows float tube which he climbs into to ride through water too deep for chest waders. (Ginny Gooch photo.)

you can begin with them. Even many of the principle tributaries will be shown. Study the country through which the river flows. Is it farming country? Mountainous? Urbanized? Wilderness or semi-wilderness? Except for an occasional smallmouth, the mountain country is more likely to provide stream fishing for trout, and the urbanized areas may be too populated — even though I've found some good bass fishing in tiny streams amazingly close to dense population centers. Wilderness is always good — if there are enough secondary roads to provide access to small streams. Personally, I like farming country. Here you will find an abundance of farm ponds to release bass into the streams and there is usually good access.

Choose the area that appeals to you, and then purchase several topographic maps of that area. You may need several to cover all of the possibilities. These maps will provide details such as farm ponds, remote roads that lead to or cross the streams, the location of farm dwellings, and other such information.

Having studied your maps, get in your automobile and do a little exploring. Locate some likely streams and get permission to fish them or to cross private property to do so. "That little stream? Sure, go ahead and fish it if you want, but there're no fish in it to amount to anything." I

131

can't remember how many times I've gotten that response. But find out for yourself. Get in the stream and fish it. You'll soon get the answer.

Mixed creels are the usual result, but in that creel there should be a good number of bass largemouths, smallmouths, or spotted. Sometimes all three, but probably most frequently the largemouth. Usually the bigmouth is the most likely possibility, but it depends on what kind of native bass fin the streams downstream.

Trout anglers often argue the merits of fishing upstream or down, but as a bass angler I catch fish either way. I usually fish with spinning tackle and make casts long enough that there is no problem of casting my shadow on the water where it will spook the fish. When you fish downstream you can't always use the current to the best advantage. Ideally, you should work your lure so it moves with the current as that is where stream bass await for much of their food. You can do this, however, by hugging one bank and casting across the stream. Let your lure swing downstream with the current to a degree, and then work it out of the current and back to you.

Working downstream is less tiring because you move with the current and not against it.

I sometimes work upstream from an access point and then back down. That way you cover the water both ways. Working upstream you can cast diagonally to either side and use the current better — but I catch bass either way. Which way you fish a stream often depends upon other considerations. For example, I much prefer to "fish through," entering the stream at an upstream access point, usually where a road crosses the stream, and continuing downstream to another road. To do this I have someone follow me to the downstream access point where I leave my automobile and then have my friend drop me off at the upstream point. You could, of course, reverse this by leaving your car upstream and working from the lower access point. It's more of a personal preference than a fishing consideration.

One thing to keep in mind about stream bass, however,

is that they like to rest with their heads facing into the current — or upstream. About the only exception to this comes when you have a swirling back eddy where the current is reversed. When viewed in this respect it become obvious that there is some advantage to fishing upstream instead of down. But you will catch bass either way.

Small streams are usually well shaded during the warm months when the foliage is full grown. On a hot summer day when the sun beams unmercifully, bouncing its rays off of the surface of a big lake onto his unprotected face, an angler soon sees the advantages of a well-shaded small stream. Step into the cool waters and you'll forget about the unrelenting heat outside the stream.

But comfort for the angler is not the only consideration during such uncomfortably hot weather. Small stream bass are more likely to cooperate than those in the big lakes. Undoubtedly boosted by the constant supply of cool, oxygen-rich water, they may feed all day. Dawn and dusk can still be prime fishing times, but I've found I can catch stream bass throughout the day. I don't have to lose sleep or miss meals to enjoy some good bass fishing.

Don't expect to catch many truly big bass in those small streams. There may be a few in the deeper pools, but a lunker is rare. But size tends to be relative. A 2-pound smallmouth in a tiny stream is a real trophy, mainly because you don't expect many bass of that size.

Because I don't expect to catch any real lunkers, I tend to drop down to ultralight spinning tackle for these bass forays. This means 4-pound test line. I've even tried 2-pound test line, but found myself losing too many fish and too many lures. I've never fished 3-pound test, but it might work. One of the advantages of the light tackle is the thin or clear water you usually encounter. The thin monofilament is less conspicuous. There's also the added joy of doing battle with the spunky bass with light, willowy tackle. Battling a feisty 2-pound bass on light tackle can be a real challenge. There are usually plenty of snags and other obstacles in most streams to increase the risk of losing a good bass if you don't handle it properly.

And don't think for a minute that those small-stream bass don't fight. Blessed with an abundance of food, cool, clean water, and plenty of oxygen, they will outfight their lake cousins. Spunk makes up for size. The fish even taste better on the table.

Finally, there is a little trick I learned long ago that can help you with your stream fishing. In one of my favorite small streams there were several pools that were too deep to wade. This meant I had to climb out of the water up a steep bank, and wade through tangles of briers and vines to continue downstream. It also meant I had to pass up some good water. A problem worth some thought.

The solution came one quiet evening while I was thumbing leisurely through a popular outdoor magazine. My eyes caught a modest advertisement by an Alabama entrepreneur, obviously a bass fisherman who had experienced the same problem I had — or similar one. He was offering for the grand sum of $9.95 a green canvas cover into which could be inserted an automobile innertube. Once inflated the combination produced a doughnut-shaped float tube with a saddle seat into which an angler could climb and float in comfort. It also had a couple of pockets for lures and other accessories — plus a couple of loops to which an angler could attach a fish stringer or other such gear. It was just what I was looking for. Got my $9.95 in the mail in a hurry and soon my float tube arrived. I bought a used innertube and I was ready for those deep pools too deep to wade through. To one of the loops I tied a piece of cord with the other end secured to my belt and allowed the float to ride along behind me as I waded and fished. Once I reached a deep hole I simply crawled in and floated through. That's one reason I'm inclined to wade downstream. Working the tube against the current would be a chore.

Incidentally, you will either need chest waders or be contented with getting wet up to your waist when you ride the float tube. You will sit in water — which might be refreshing on a hot summer day.

Bass fishing wouldn't be the same if I didn't have a small stream to fish.

Chapter XV
Rivers

The author wades the Umpqua River in Oregon for smallmouth bass.
Ginny Gooch photo.

Anglers new to fishing rivers for bass tend to overlook possibly the most important element of such fishing, the current. Regardless of its size, every river has a current. Figure that out and you are well along toward becoming a river bass angler. Veteran river anglers are experts at it. In the large slow-flowing rivers the current may be all but imperceptible, but it's there.

Tidal rivers also have currents, but they are tidal currents that flow in and out twice a day. There are a number of secrets to successfully fishing tidal rivers, and we will get to them later.

135

For our purposes I will define a river as discussed here as a stream too large and too deep to wade. There may be small sections of it you can wade, riffles or shoals, for example, but such fishing will be extremely limited. To effectively fish a river as we are defining it here you need a boat, one such as discussed in Chapter V. For a fast smallmouth river a canoe is almost perfect, though many good river fishermen prefer jon boats. A motor is probably not needed though a small one might be helpful. Usually there is enough current to keep the boat or canoe moving, with at least one angler using a paddle to keep the craft on course and to adjust its speed to an acceptable rate for fishing. For slower flatlands rivers where there is not enough current to provide acceptable speed, a small motor is usually needed.

Access to the river comes first. Thanks to the fisheries agencies in most good fishing states, public access in the form of launching ramps and automobile parking space is found on the major rivers. On some, particularly the smaller ones, you may have to resort to highway crossings or private land to get access.

A canoe is a fine craft for fishing fast smallmouth bass rivers.

Ideally a river should be fished through — from one access to another — and this usually means fishing downstream. Working a canoe or jon boat upstream through rapids and shoals is tough and all but impossible. The ideal way is to use the current and float fish — downstream. This means running a shuttle, and you need two automobiles, unless there is shuttle service available. Both vehicles are driven to the downstream access point where you will end your trip and take your boat out of the river. Park one vehicle there. Then all anglers and the boat travel to the upstream access point in the other vehicle. The second automobile is parked there. At the end of the trip, you will have to return by road and pick it up. If both vehicles have the capacity to carry the boat or canoe, that's the end of the shuttle. Otherwise the upstream vehicle will have to be driven back downstream to pick up the boat or canoe. Sound complicated? Not really.

Another approach is to have someone, friend or spouse, meet you at the downstream access point at a designated time. That, however, ties you down. You might have to pass up some good fishing in order to make the downstream appointment.

Another way to fish such streams is to launch at an access point and make a run upstream for a float back to that access. This is ideal for a brief fishing trip that may take just a couple of hours. You need a small outboard for this type of trip. I live approximately three miles from a reasonably good smallmouth bass stream that also often gives up some largemouths. Occasionally, when I have just a couple of hours to fish, I'll load my light aluminum boat in the back of my truck, and drive to the river. I can launch the boat by myself. I then clamp on my little 3 1/2-horsepower outboard and run up the river as far as I can before an impossible rapids blocks further travel.I work that fast water thoroughly before yielding to the current and drifting back downstream — fishing as I go. I always catch bass on those little trips.

To tackle this subject let's break rivers down into smallmouth streams, spotted bass streams, flatlands rivers, and tidal rivers.

137

I suspect that across America the smallmouth fishermen predominate when it comes to fishing rivers. Good smallmouth rivers are found in just about every corner of the country. They are found in both the Atlantic and Pacific Ocean drainage systems as well as in Middle America. Over the years I've caught smallmouth bass in such eastern rivers as the James and Shenandoah in Virginia, the Umpqua in Oregon, and the Tennessee in Tennessee and Alabama. And these are just a sample of what's available. Smallmouth rivers are found from Maine to California and from Minnesota south to Texas.

Smallmouth rivers typically are reasonably fast with rapids, riffles, shoals, long stretches of shallows, and some deep pools where the big bass like to spend most of their time. Early and late in the day I like to concentrate on the shallows and shoals and the water at the tails of rapids. That's where the fish tend to feed. In the middle of the day I fish deep, working those deep pools carefully. For the shallows it's hard to improve on surface lures such as the Tiny Torpedo or shallow running diving-floating lures such as the Rapala. I allow the Rapala to float a lot, twitching it occasionally. For the deep pools crankbaits and spinnerbaits are good, but in recent years the various plastic lures have become popular and effective.

When you float a river, you move with the current and it's difficult to work your lure with the current unless you cast back upstream. This is possible occasionally, but the combination of the moving craft and the retrieve of the lure tends to move the lure too rapidly. Keep this in mind when you make this cast. As we've already learned, stream fish like to face upstream into the current which brings them much of their food. Casting downstream ignores this concept.

Ideally, the cast should be made across or diagonally upstream or down and the lure allowed to move with the current. You can do this by carefully working your lure across the current. It's highly effective. An exception comes when the bass are feeding on minnows, breaking the

138

Stacey King fishes an Ozark smallmouth bass stream from a jon boat, fine for floating rivers.

water and creating a ruckus on the water. Nothing excites a smallmouth angler more. In such a situation it makes little difference which way you work your lure. Just make it look like a frantic or crippled minnow — either fluttering on the surface or moving beneath it.

All kinds of obstacles break the flow of the current in a fast river. Boulders are probably the most prevalent, and they are a good place for a bass to rest out of the relentless current. It can rest quietly and at the same time watch the current on either side of the boulder for the food it sweeps by. A flick of its fins, a quick dash into the current, and it has a tasty tidbit. Recognizing this habit of the fish, the angler can take advantage of it by casting slightly upstream of a boulder, working his lure so it is positioned just above it, and letting it float by in the current. It is probably the most effective technique for catching river smallmouths.

The combination of boulders or rocks and vegetation is attractive to smallmouth bass. Both offer it food, and lures worked in this combination of cover or structure can be highly productive.

On warm summer days as the sun climbs toward the heavens and sends its hot rays beaming down on the river, smallmouths tend to seek the cover of streamside shade — well foliaged brush and trees. A surface lure shot back beneath that foliage and allowed to drop gently on the water is almost sure to get attention. It's a good technique for midday fishing. To do it successfully, however, you have to perfect your side cast, sending your lure skimming just above the surface of the water.

Smallmouth bass rivers tend to be clear much of the time, and for that reason I like a light line for the thin water. I've lost some good smallmouths on 4-pound test line, but I still use it if the water is unusually clear. I suspect, however, that 6-pound test is a safer choice. And fish it on a light spinning rod with a flexible tip that absorbs much of the shock of a fighting fish. This protects the light line.

Spotted bass also like reasonably fast streams, and you may find them in the same water with smallmouth bass. Generally, however, good spotted bass streams are a bit slower — more gentle than that preferred by the small-mouth. I've caught the fish in lakes as well as stream, but most bass anglers probably have less experience with the spotted bass than with the other two.

The fishing techniques already discussed with respect to the faster smallmouth and spotted bass streams generally apply to flatlands rivers. There is still plenty of current in the slower rivers, but it is not as fast. Rapids and riffles are limited — if they exist at all. There will be plenty of shallow water, however, and usually more deep water.

Many of these flatlands rivers eventually become tidal streams if they flow eventually into the oceans along the several coasts. Possibly the major difference between these rivers and the tidal ones is the absence of tides.

It's possible to float these rivers much as you would a fast smallmouth bass stream, but doing so can be painfully slow. At the minimum you should have an electric motor to move you along. A small gasoline motor is better, however, particularly if you find yourself far from your take-out point late in the day and want to speed up your progress.

Launching your boat and running a good distance upstream to float back is more feasible on these streams where you don't have to run against a strong current or though fast rapids. For the lone angler this is probably the best approach.

Smallmouth bass are rare in these slow-flowing rivers, but you may find good spotted bass fishing in some of them. Primarily, however, the flatlands streams are largemouth waters, some of the very best to be found. Frankly, I prefer rivers over the big reservoirs. Even in the slow rivers the bass tend to live with the currents and I find them generally a more streamlined fish. No potbellies. Because of the continuous currents, they enjoy more oxygen and I suspect the food base is better. A river bank is seldom far away and this means more feeding opportunities.

Don't forget we are still thinking currents with bass resting and facing into it to look for food. Keep this in mind as you fish. Casting upstream is more feasible now because of the slower current. Do this and you are working your lure toward the bass facing upstream. This offers an advantage in that the fish is more likely to spot it. Don't, however, overlook the effectiveness of a lure cast across the current and worked slowly across it.

While there is plenty of deep water where the bass may hole up at certain times of the day, the flatlands river bass are probably more likely to be found throughout the river much of the day. They also like the banks where there is cover and food. I spend a lot of time fishing the banks, swinging back and forth across the river if one bank looks better than the other. And I like to alternate between topwater and deep-running lures more often than when fishing the faster smallmouth streams.

Over the years the flatlands streams have received more than their fair share of pollutants, but thankfully that is being addressed by all levels of government and numerous private groups. Our rivers generally are in better condition than they were in years past. There is still room for improvement, but in the meantime they are capable of furnishing some fine bass fishing.

Finally, let's look at tidal rivers. These interesting and unique waters can provide some fantastic bass fishing. It is largemouth bass fishing just about exclusively. The tides, which create most of the current, are the key to successful bass fishing.

Fix this firmly in mind. Since bass like to rest facing into the current, tidal river bass change positions four times each 24 hours. When the tide comes in they face down-stream, but when it goes out they face upstream. And remember the tides change four times a day, flooding twice and ebbing twice.

Another key to successful tidal river bass fishing is knowing when the tides peak — at the low period as well as high. Fishing can be deadly slow during those periods between the change of tide. The tide reaches flood stage and it holds there for an hour or so. The same is true of the

Outdoor writer George Huber checks a lure while fishing the Rivanna River, a Virginia smallmouth stream.

low tide. Check you local tidal tables and know when these periods occur. Fishing is very slow at both times.

Like all river bass, tidal river bass like moving water. This means currents, so plan your fishing so you will be there when the tide is moving. Some anglers like an ebb tide because it draws water out of the ditches and shallows forcing the forage fish into open water where they are more vulnerable to feeding bass. I lean toward this period, but the incoming tide floods the flats making them available to bass that move in for the food the flood tide makes available.

143

Actually both conditions are good. You can't miss regardless of which tide you fish. And dawn and dusk lose their significance on tidal rivers.

Tides tend to pass reasonably fast. This limits the fishing tide at any particularly spot in the river. "I prolong my fishing time by moving with the tide," said Woo Daves, a highly successful professional bass angler who fishes the James River in Virginia a lot.

The usual practices of using the currents apply to tidal river bass fishing. Just remember that the currents move downstream as well as up. With this in mind watch for obstacles that break the current. You won't find many boulders in most tidal streams, though I've seen them in west coast streams and in some of the Maine tidal streams. Generally, though, you have to look to other obstacles. Piles of debris, stumps, old logs, duck blinds, and the like break the current and provide a place for bass to rest out of the current. Just remember to cast up-current from such obstacles and allow your lure to sweep slowly by.

The rivers of this country provide some of the finest bass fishing in America and much of it is amazingly accessible.

Chapter XVI
Reservoirs

Even at dawn the heat is making itself felt. "It'll be hot out there on the water," you say to yourself as you prepare for a day of summer fishing. Hopefully, before that day is up there'll be some nice bass cooling in your ice chest.

But that's a lot of water and it all looks alike - flat with mists rising here and there. No landmarks, nothing to indicate where the fish will be. Still worse, out there in the middle of the giant reservoir the water is almost 40 feet deep. Where to begin this day of fishing that held so much promise when you planned it?

That's a typical reaction of a bass angler fresh to reservoir fishing. No bass water can be more puzzling.

The big reservoirs that have sprung up across America since the end of World War II have revolutionized bass fishing in this country. Many have been built as flood control measures, other to provide electrical power, and some for recreation. Regardless of the intent, these impoundments have provided millions of acres of bass fishing water that did not exist a half century ago. Size? Anywhere from a couple of thousand acres to 100,000 or more. Big water, and anglers have flocked to the fishing this additional water offers. Access is excellent on most of them, usually public access points and concrete launching ramps provided by either federal or state agencies.

But where do you fish out there on all of that flat water? The angler who can't answer that question is licked before he begins fishing.

A good way to begin is in your living room at home. Get a good topographic map of the lake. Most tackle shops in the vicinity of a big lake have them. Study it thoroughly.

Don't try to fish the whole reservoir or giant lake, break it down.

The author anchored off a point and fished its slopes to get this action.
Ginny Gooch photo

Look for contour lines that will show depths at various parts of the lake. Note the creeks — now inundated of course. Make mental notes of ridges that run into the lake — and how far they continue under the water. Check out the major feeder stream or streams, the river or rivers that were impounded to form the lake, and check the location of all smaller feeder streams. A grasp of these features can lead you to better fishing. By all means check out the shallows. They could provide your first fish. And take this map with you when you first fish the lake. It can prove invaluable.

Are there fishing guides to the lake, inexpensive soft-cover books or booklets? By all means pick one up. And don't mind asking questions. The responses you get will be varied, but some will be helpful. Marina operators, other anglers, and conservation officers are the usual source of information. Or tackle shops. If you are successful, they know you will return and become a steady customer. They will help.

Now you are ready to fish, but don't try to fish the whole lake. Break it down using the information you have found in studying the map. Do you want to fish a creek that enters the lake? It's always a good bet in hot weather. The water is cooler there and the bass find plenty of food. The advantage to the angler is that the water is usually relatively shallow when compared to the main body of water. Your little boat might be equipped with a depth finder even if it doesn't have a fish finder. The depth finder can be helpful in informing you of the depth of the water. With that knowledge you are in a better position to know how to fish the water, how deeply to run your spinnerbait, for example. There may even be some current in the creek, particularly upstream near the top of the impounded water.

There are numerous other possibilities. Let's take a look at them. And don't try to fish the whole lake. Break it down into the great variety of possibilities.

Fishing the shallows is always a good possibility for the angler who has never fished a big lake before. Forget about all of the water out there and concentrate on a patch of shallow water. How to you locate it? Look at that map you studied prior to your trip. The contour lines will show you. Is there a stump field? If so plan on giving it plenty of attention. This is the remains of a hardwood forests that was logged before the lake was built. You often find this kind of water in lakes — and long after the lake was first formed. Wood under water lasts for years. Working around those old stumps can be highly productive and it's water you can often reach in a small boat.

Shallows are generally close to shore, an advantage for the angler who does not own a fast bass boat. They may be the flats or bottom lands along an inundated creek, or it might be the land upstream from the forks of a pair of inundated creeks. The contour map should provide this information. Or the shallows may be out in the lake, the crown of an inundated hill. Such an area may be small because of the nature of hilltops, but even so it could hold some good bass.

Fishing the shallows is a good bet for the beginning angler because he does not have to attempt to figure out the mysterious depths found out in the lake. Nor does he probably have the electronic gear to enable him to do so. Those shallows are much easier to fish because the bass has more limited depth in which to feed. The shallows are also good because they can be a rich feeding ground for bass and other fish.

The immediate problem the angler has to deal with is not spooking the bass in the shallow water. If the water is very clear, this is tough to avoid. Long casts help, and use the lightest line possible. Also try to avoid casting your shadow on the water — particularly in the direction you are fishing. The best solution, however, is to time your trip so as to take advantage of natural conditions that help mask your approach. Dawn and dusk are ideal times. Before the sun has touched the water or after it leaves. Night is even better if you don't dislike fishing after dark. Add the fact that bass enter those shadows to feed, and you have another reason for being there at night or early or late in the day.

Flooded timber in big reservoirs is usually good and easy to fish.

Another condition that favors the angler fishing the shallows is muddy or dingy water. The visibility is limited then and the angler is not as conspicuous to the feeding fish. Another weather condition that helps is a good breeze that keeps a good ripple on the surface. This also breaks up the angler's outline, making him less conspicuous to the feeding bass.

Shallows are easier to fish because of the limited water. A popping or gurgling surface lure can be highly effective when the bass are in the shallows. Try it first and then shift to something else if it doesn't produce.

Another piece of water worth considering is that in the creeks. We are thinking now of that broad stretch of water at the confluence of the creek and the lake plus the water within the old banks of the creek. You will usually find a good cove where the water begins to spread out. Here you have a situation that attracts bass - the colder, invigorating water pouring in from the creek and plenty of food that drifts in from the creek. You also have the advantage of a more concentrated piece of water to work. You don't have to search as far for the bass. If your map shows a creek with a public launching ramp on or near it, by all means check it out. Such water is convenient and you can get on it quickly even with a small boat. Such water is particularly attractive on a hot summer day. There is usually a good deal of shade that is welcome to the angler as well as the bass.

Of course there is always the shoreline. Fish frequent the shorelines even during the warmer months, though they do so more frequently early and late in the day and at night.

Bass also seek the shore for spawning. Early in the season, usually March and April, depending upon the part of the country you live in or are fishing, fishing the shorelines can be very productive. "They are almost too vulnerable then," said one fisheries biologist.

The spring spawning season is a good time to fish spinnerbaits among the willows and other shoreline vegetation. The water is usually high then flooding willow flats and other areas that will be exposed later in the year. This is shallow fishing for the most part — shallow- running underwater lures.

An often overlooked, but easily located fishing area, is the boat dock. These structures line most of the big lakes, and they offer a good opportunity for the angler new to big waters. Bass seek boat docks mostly for protection from the sun, but they often find food there. Some of that food is inadvertently placed there by the owner of the dock. He may dump his minnow bucket before heading for home, for example, or even a can of worms. Docks also attract insects and small fish. I attended a major bass fishing tournament several years ago and watched an enterprising angler place second in the tournament by fishing boat docks. "People probably thought I was praying," he joked. He spent much of his time down on his knees attempting to cast his lure back beneath the docks. He happened to be fishing a river that time, but reservoir docks are equally as good. You may want to pass up docks occupied by the owner, but on most lakes there are many of them in front of unoccupied cottages. Take advantage of them. Their condition doesn't matter. Some may be brand new whereas others may be all but rotten. It makes no difference to the bass.

Going back to natural cover, check that map again and note the presence of ridges that disappear into the lake. They may begin as ridges a good distance from the lake, but eventually enter the lake and disappear beneath the surface. Some continue well into the lake while others end as sharp points near the shore. It is those sharp points that I like. You don't really have to check a map to spot them. They are obvious, but the map will show where they exist in the lake and the nearest launching ramp to some good ones.

I like to work those points out. The bottom of the lake descends rather rapidly, but you can walk a lure down those points and get good results. Crankbait, spinnerbait, or some other lure. Just bounce if off of the bottom. And work both sides of a point. If one doesn't produce maybe the other will.

I was fishing Fontana Lake in North Carolina several springs ago and not enjoying too much success. Then a friend gave me a tip. "Go up Eagle Creek," he said. "Anchor your boat on the second point and cast out at one o'clock." I did so and caught a nice smallmouth on my very first cast.

While it's not true of all big reservoirs, you will find dead and standing timber in some of them. One I recall is Toledo Bend on the Louisiana-Texas border. Typically a river basin is cleared of timber before it is impounded. This often leaves stump flats, but rarely standing timber. You don't need a depth finder to locate that timber. Another such lake is Lake Marion of the famous Santee-Cooper lakes in South Carolina. I don't know why the timber was left in those two giant lakes, but the important thing is that it is there and it can serve an angler well. Sure you can lose

A jon boat can be used on large lakes if you don't venture too far from shore where you won't have the equipment to locate the bass.

lures when a big one wraps you around a tree trunk or the branch of a tree, but you'll catch enough bass to make up for the loss. Such old timber attracts insects, bait fish and all kinds of food for a hungry bass.

Today fisheries managers are even deliberately leaving standing timber in lakes to improve the quality of the fishing.

Even launching ramps, public or private, offer fishing opportunities. In this modern day of bass tournaments every weekend, anglers often weigh in their bass and then release them at the nearest launching ramp. Those fish tend to hang around for awhile. I once watched a professional bass angler take his limit fishing around a private launching ramp. I don't know whether he violated any rules, but he took his fish in, weighed them, and turned them over to the state fisheries agency. They were later released back into the water in good condition.

Most major bodies of inland water contain riprap, man-made structure off rocks or stones that controls erosion on a bank or possibly even seals off a soft bottom. Regardless of the objective, ripraps also offer good fishing. The better ones slope sharply in the water, and they can be fished much as you would a point as described above. There is riprap around bridge abutments. The thing about riprap is that it is easily located. No need for electronic gear as most of it is at least partially above the surface of the water.

Bridges. Most big lakes are crossed by several major highways or secondary roads. They offer shade from the sun, some riprap around the abutments, and the abutments themselves that are attractive to fish. Generally speaking the bridges are convenient to launching ramps because they themselves are of necessity near the highways or roads that bridge the lakes. Like the bridges they support, the abutments also cast shadows that appeal to bass on a hot summer day. They also attract various kinds of food.

I once fished a big Kentucky reservoir with a friend and relative, and when we motored into the dock late one day, we found the owner bemoaning the loss of a pet. "We had a pet bass here that we've been feeding and keeping alive for years, and today one of our anglers caught it and cleaned it before we had a chance to tell him about the fish. He was fishing off the dock." I wouldn't have wanted to be in that angler's shoes, but the little story goes a long way toward pointing out that if you break a big lake down into sections you can catch bass without a lot of electronic gear and a fast bass boat. Anglers were doing so long before such equipment came on the market.

Don't allow the inability to finance a modern bass boat keep you off the water. You can catch bass without it.